The Spanish Friar by John Dryden

Or, The Double Discovery

—Alterna revisens
Lasit, et in solido rursus fortuna locavit.
—*VIRG.*

John Dryden was born on August 9th, 1631 in the village rectory of Aldwincle near Thrapston in Northamptonshire. As a boy Dryden lived in the nearby village of Titchmarsh, Northamptonshire. In 1644 he was sent to Westminster School as a King's Scholar.

Dryden obtained his BA in 1654, graduating top of the list for Trinity College, Cambridge that year.

Returning to London during The Protectorate, Dryden now obtained work with Cromwell's Secretary of State, John Thurloe.

At Cromwell's funeral on 23 November 1658 Dryden was in the company of the Puritan poets John Milton and Andrew Marvell. The setting was to be a sea change in English history. From Republic to Monarchy and from one set of lauded poets to what would soon become the Age of Dryden.

The start began later that year when Dryden published the first of his great poems, Heroic Stanzas (1658), a eulogy on Cromwell's death.

With the Restoration of the Monarchy in 1660 Dryden celebrated in verse with Astraea Redux, an authentic royalist panegyric.

With the re-opening of the theatres after the Puritan ban, Dryden began to also write plays. His first play, The Wild Gallant, appeared in 1663 but was not successful. From 1668 on he was contracted to produce three plays a year for the King's Company, in which he became a shareholder. During the 1660s and '70s, theatrical writing was his main source of income.

In 1667, he published Annus Mirabilis, a lengthy historical poem which described the English defeat of the Dutch naval fleet and the Great Fire of London in 1666. It established him as the pre-eminent poet of his generation, and was crucial in his attaining the posts of Poet Laureate (1668) and then historiographer royal (1670).

This was truly the Age of Dryden, he was the foremost English Literary figure in Poetry, Plays, translations and other forms.

In 1694 he began work on what would be his most ambitious and defining work as translator, The Works of Virgil (1697), which was published by subscription. It was a national event.

John Dryden died on May 12th, 1700, and was initially buried in St. Anne's cemetery in Soho, before being exhumed and reburied in Westminster Abbey ten days later.

Index of Contents
THE SPANISH FRIAR. AN INTRODUCTION
TO THE RIGHT HONOURABLE JOHN, LORD HAUGHTON
PROLOGUE
DRAMATIS PERSONÆ
THE SPANISH FRIAR or, THE DOUBLE DISCOVERY
ACT I
SCENE I
SCENE II
ACT II
SCENE I.—The Queen's Antechamber
SCENE II—A Chamber. A Table and Wine Set Out
SCENE III.—A Chamber
ACT III
SCENE I.—The Street
SCENE II.—Elvira's Chamber
SCENE III.—A Bed Chamber
ACT IV
SCENE I.—Before Gomez's Door
SCENE II.—The Court
ACT V
SCENE I.—A Bed-Chamber
SCENE II.—The Palace-Yard. Drums and Trumpets Within
EPILOGUE. BY A FRIEND OF THE AUTHOR'S.
John Dryden – A Short Biography
John Dryden – A Concise Bibliography

THE SPANISH FRIAR. AN INTRODUCTION

The Spanish Friar, or the Double Discovery, is one of the best and most popular of our poet's dramatic efforts. The plot is, as Johnson remarks, particularly happy, for the coincidence and coalition of the tragic and comic plots. The grounds for this eminent critic's encomium will be found to lie more deep than appears at first sight. It was, indeed, a sufficiently obvious connection, to make the gay Lorenzo an officer of the conquering army, and attached to the person of Torrismond. This expedient could hardly have escaped the invention of the most vulgar playwright, that ever dovetailed tragedy and comedy together. The felicity of Dryden's plot, therefore, does not consist in the ingenuity of his original conception, but in the minutely artificial strokes, by which the reader is perpetually reminded of the dependence of the one part of the play on the other. These are so frequent, and appear so very natural, that the comic plot, instead of diverting our attention from the tragic business, recalls it to our mind by constant and unaffected allusion. No great event happens in the higher region of the camp or court, that has not some indirect influence upon the intrigues of Lorenzo and Elvira; and the part which the gallant is called upon to act in the revolution that winds up the tragic interest, while it is highly in character, serves to bring the catastrophe of both parts of the play under the eye of the spectator, at one and the same time. Thus much seemed necessary to explain the felicity of combination, upon which Dryden justly valued himself, and which Johnson sanctioned by his high commendation. But, although artfully conjoined, the different departments of this tragi-comedy are separate subjects of critical remark.

The comic part of the Spanish Friar, as it gives the first title to the play, seems to claim our first attention. Indeed, some precedence is due to it in another point of view; for, though the tragic scenes may be matched in All for Love, Don Sebastian, and else where, the Spanish Friar contains by far the most happy of Dryden's comic effusions. It has, comparatively speaking, this high claim to commendation, that, although the intrigue is licentious, according to the invariable licence of the age, the language is, in general, free from the extreme and disgusting coarseness, which our author too frequently mistook for wit, or was contented to substitute in its stead. The liveliness and even brilliancy of the dialogue, shows that Dryden, from the stores of his imagination, could, when he pleased, command that essential requisite of comedy; and that, if he has seldom succeeded, it was only because he mistook the road, or felt difficulty in travelling it. The character of Dominic is of that broadly ludicrous nature, which was proper to the old comedy. It would be difficult to show an ordinary conception more fully brought out. He is, like Falstaff, a compound of sensuality and talent, finely varied by the professional traits with which it suited the author's purpose to adorn his character. Such an addition was, it is true, more comic than liberal; but Dryden, whose constant dislike to the clerical order glances out in many of his performances, was not likely to be scrupulous, when called upon to pourtray one of their members in his very worst colours. To counterbalance the Friar's scandalous propensities of every sort, and to render him an object of laughter, rather than abhorrence, the author has gifted this reprobate churchman with a large portion of wit; by means of which, and by a ready presence of mind, always indicative of energy, he preserves an ascendence over the other characters, and escapes detection and disgrace, until poetical justice, and the conclusion of the play, called for his punishment. We have a natural indulgence for an amusing libertine; and, I believe, that, as most readers commiserate the disgrace of Falstaff, a few may be found to wish that Dominic's penance had been of a nature more decent and more theatrical than the poet has assigned him[1]. From the dedication, as well as the prologue, it appears that Dryden, however contrary to his sentiments at a future period, was, at present, among those who held up to contempt and execration the character of the Roman catholic priesthood. By one anonymous lampoon, this is ascribed to a temporary desertion of the court party, in resentment for the loss, or discontinuance of his pension. This allowance, during the pressure upon the Exchequer, was, at least, irregularly paid, of which Dryden repeatedly complains, and particularly in a letter to the Earl of Rochester. But the hardship was owing entirely to the poverty of the public purse; and, when the anonymous libeller affirms, that Dryden's pension was withdrawn, on account of his share in the Essay on Satire, he only shows that his veracity is on a level with his poverty[2]. The truth seems to be, that Dryden partook in some degree of the general ferment which the discovery of the Popish Plot had excited; and we may easily suppose him to have done so without any impeachment to his monarchial tenets, since North himself admits, that at the first opening of the plot, the chiefs of the loyal party joined in the cry. Indeed, that mysterious transaction had been investigated by none more warmly than by Danby, the king's favourite minister, and a high favourer of the prerogative. Even when writing Absalom and Achitophel, our author by no means avows an absolute disbelief of the whole plot, while condemning the extraordinary exaggerations, by which it had been rendered the means of much bloodshed and persecution[3]. It seems, therefore, fair to believe, that, without either betraying or disguising his own principles, he chose, as a popular subject for the drama, an attack upon an obnoxious priesthood, whom he, in common with all the nation, believed to have been engaged in the darkest intrigues against the king and government. I am afraid that this task was the more pleasing, from that prejudice against the clergy, of all countries and religions, which, as already noticed, our author displays, in common with other wits of that licentious age[4]. The character of the Spanish Friar was not, however, forgotten, when Dryden became a convert to the Roman Catholic persuasion; and, in many instances, as well as in that just quoted, it was assumed as the means of fixing upon him a charge of inconsistency in politics, and versatility in religion[5].

The tragic part of the "Spanish Friar" has uncommon merit. The opening of the Drama, and the picture of a besieged town in the last extremity, is deeply impressive, while the description of the noise of the night attack, and the gradual manner in which the intelligence of its success is communicated, arrests the attention, and prepares expectation for the appearance of the hero, with all the splendour which ought to attend the principal character in tragedy. The subsequent progress of the plot is liable to a capital objection, from the facility with which the queen, amiable and virtuous, as we are bound to suppose her, consents to the murder of the old dethroned monarch. We question if the operation of any motive, however powerful, could have been pleaded with propriety, in apology for a breach of theatrical decorum, so gross, and so unnatural. But, in fact, the queen is only actuated by a sort of reflected ambition, a desire to secure to her lover a crown, which she thought in danger; but which, according to her own statement, she only valued on his account. This is surely too remote and indirect a motive, to urge a female to so horrid a crime. There is also something vilely cold-hearted, in her attempt to turn the guilt and consequences of her own crime upon Bertran, who, whatever faults he might have to others, was to the queen no otherwise obnoxious, than because the victim of her own inconstancy. The gallant, virtuous, and enthusiastic character of Torrismond, must be allowed, in some measure, to counterbalance that of his mistress, however unhappily he has placed his affections. But the real excellence of these scenes consists less in peculiarity of character, than in the vivacity and power of the language, which, seldom sinking into vulgarity, or rising into bombast, maintains the mixture of force and dignity, best adapted to the expression of tragic passion. Upon the whole, as the comic part of this play is our author's master-piece in comedy, the tragic plot may be ranked with his very best efforts of that kind, whether in "Don Sebastian," or "All for Love."

The "Spanish Friar" appears to have been brought out shortly after Mr Thynne's murder, which is alluded to in the Prologue, probably early in 1681-2. The whimsical caricature, which it presented to the public, in Father Dominic, was received with rapture by the prejudiced spectators, who thought nothing could be exaggerated in the character of a Roman Catholic priest. Yet, the satire was still more severe in the first edition, and afterwards considerably softened[6]. It was, as Dryden himself calls it, a Protestant play; and certainly, as Jeremy Collier somewhere says, was rare Protestant diversion, and much for the credit of the Reformation. Accordingly, the "Spanish Friar" was the only play prohibited by James II. after his accession; an interdict, which may be easily believed no way disagreeable to the author, now a convert to the Roman church. It is very remarkable, that, after the Revolution, it was the first play represented by order of queen Mary, and honoured with her presence; a choice, of which she had abundant reason to repent, as the serious part of the piece gave as much scope for malicious application against herself, as the comic against the religion of her father[7].

Footnotes

1. Collier remarks the injustice of punishing the agent of Lorenzo's vice, while he was himself brought off with flying colours. He observes, "'Tis not the fault which is corrected, but the priest. The author's discipline is seldom without a bias. He commonly gives the laity the pleasure of an ill action, and the clergy the punishment." View of the Immorality and Profaneness of the Stage, p. 100.

2. To satire next thy talent was addressed,
Fell foul on all thy friends among the rest;

Nay, even thy royal patron was not spared,
But an obscene, a sauntering wretch declared.
Thy loyal libel we can still produce,
Beyond example, and beyond excuse.
O strange return, to a forgiving king,
(But the warmed viper wears the greatest sting,)
For pension lost, and justly without doubt;
When servants snarl we ought to kick them out.
They that disdain their benefactor's bread.
No longer ought by bounty to be fed.
That lost, the visor changed, you turn about,
And straight a true-blue protestant crept out.
The Friar now was writ, and some will say,
They smell a malcontent through all the play.
The papist too was damned, unfit for trust,
Called treacherous, shameless, profligate, unjust,
And kingly power thought arbitrary lust.
This lasted till thou didst thy pension gain,
And that changed both thy morals and thy strain.
The Laureat, 24th October, 1678.

3. From hence began that plot, the nation's curse,
Bad in itself, but represented worse.
Raised in extremes, and in extremes decryed,
With oaths affirmed, with dying vows denied;
Nor weighed nor winnowed by the multitude,
But swallowed in the mass unchewed and crude.
Some truth there was, but dashed and bruised with lies,
To please the fools, and puzzle all the wise.
Succeeding times did equal folly call.
Believing nothing, or believing all.

4. "Thus we see," says Collier, "how hearty these people are in their ill-will; how they attack religion under every form, and pursue the priesthood through all the subdivisions of opinion. Neither Jews nor Heathens, Turk nor Christians, Rome nor Geneva, church nor conventicle, can escape them. They are afraid lest virtue should have any quarters, undisturbed conscience any corner to retire to, or God worshipped in any place." Short View, &c. p. 110.

5. "I have read somewhere in Mons. Rapin's Reflections sur la Poetique, that a certain Venetian nobleman, Andrea Naugeria by name, was wont every year to sacrifice a Martial to the manes of Catullus: In imitation of this, a celebrated poet, in the preface before the Spanish Friar, is pleased to acquaint the world, that he has indignation enough to burn a Bussy D'Amboys, annually, to the memory of Ben Jonson. Since the modern ceremony, of offering up one author at the altar of another, is likely to advance into a fashion; and having already the authority of two such great men to recommend it, the courteous reader may be pleased to take notice, that the author of the following dialogue is resolved, (God willing) on the festival of the Seven Sleepers, as long as he lives, to sacrifice the Hind and Panther to the memory of Mr Quarels and John Bunyan: Or, if a writer that has notoriously contradicted himself, and espoused the quarrel of two different parties, may be considered under two distinct characters, he

designs to deliver up the author of the Hind and Panther, to be lashed severely by, and to beg pardon of, the worthy gentleman that wrote the Spanish Friar, and the Religion Laici." The reason of Mr Bayes' changing his religion. Preface.

6. "The Revolter," a tragi-comedy, 1687, p. 29.

7. It is impossible to avoid transcribing the whole account of this representation, with some other curious particulars, contained in a letter from the earl of Nottingham, published by Sir John Dalrymple, from a copy given him by the bishop of Dromore; and also inserted by Mr Malone in his third volume of Dryden's prose works.

"I am loth to send blank paper by a carrier, but am rather willing to send some of the tattle of the town, than nothing at all; which will at least serve for an hour's chat,—and then convert the scrawl to its proper use.

"The only day her Majesty gave herself the diversion of a play, and that on which she designed to see another, has furnished the town with discourse for near a month. The choice of the play was THE SPANISH FRIAR, the only play forbid by the late King, Some unhappy expressions, among which those that follow, put her in some disorder, and forced her to hold up her fan, and often look behind her, and call for her palatine and hood, and any thing she could next think of; while those who were in the pit before her, turned their heads over their shoulders, and all in general directed their looks towards her, whenever their fancy led them to make any application of what was said. In one place, where the queen of Arragon is going to church in procession, 'tis said by a spectator, 'Very good; she usurps the throne, keeps the old king in prison, and, at the same time, is praying for a blessing on her army;'—And when said, 'That 'tis observed at Court, who weeps, and who wears black for good king Sancho's death,' 'tis said, 'Who is that, that can flatter a Court like this? Can I sooth tyranny? seem pleas'd to see my Royal Master murthered; his crown usurped; a distaff in the throne?'—And 'What title has this queen, but lawless force; and force must pull her down'—Twenty more things are said, which may be wrested to what they were never designed: but however, the observations then made furnished the town with talk, till something else happened, which gave it much occasion for discourse; for another play being ordered to be acted, the queen came not, being taken up with other diversion. She dined with Mrs Gradens, the famous woman in the hall, that sells fine laces and head-dresses; from thence she went to the Jew's, that sells Indian things; to Mrs Ferguson's, De Vett's, Mrs Harrison's, and other Indian houses; but not to Mrs Potter's, though in her way; which caused Mrs Potter to say, that she might as well have hoped for that honour as others, considering that the whole design of bringing the queen and king was managed at her house, and the consultations held there; so that she might as well have thrown away a little money in raffling there, as well as at the other houses: but it seems that my lord Devonshire has got Mrs Potter to be laundress: she has not much countenance of the queen, her daughter still keeping the Indian house her mother had. The same day the queen went to one Mrs Wise's, a famous woman for telling fortunes, but could not prevail with her to tell anything; though to others she has been very true, and has foretold that king James shall came in again, and the duke of Norfolk shall lose his head: the last, I suppose, will naturally be the consequence of the first. These things, however innocent, have passed the censure of the town: and, besides a private reprimand given, the king gave one in public; saying to the queen, that he heard she dined at a bawdy-house, and desired the next time she went, he might go. She said, she had done nothing but what the late queen had done. He asked her, if she meant to make her, her example. More was said on this occasion than ever was known before; but it was borne with all the submission of a good wife, who leaves all to the direction of the k—, and diverts herself with walking six or seven miles *a-day, and looking after her buildings, making of fringes, and such like innocent things; and does not meddle in government, though she has better title to do it than the late queen had."*

TO THE RIGHT HONOURABLE JOHN, LORD HAUGHTON[1].

MY LORD,

When I first designed this play, I found, or thought I found, somewhat so moving in the serious part of it, and so pleasant in the comic, as might deserve a more than ordinary care in both; accordingly, I used the best of my endeavour, in the management of two plots, so very different from each other, that it was not perhaps the talent of every writer to have made them of a piece. Neither have I attempted other plays of the same nature, in my opinion, with the same judgment, though with like success. And though many poets may suspect themselves for the fondness and partiality of parents to their youngest children, yet I hope I may stand exempted from this rule, because I know myself too well to be ever satisfied with my own conceptions, which have seldom reached to those ideas that I had within me; and consequently, I may presume to have liberty to judge when I write more or less pardonably, as an ordinary marksman may know certainly when he shoots less wide at what he aims. Besides, the care and pains I have bestowed on this, beyond my other tragi-comedies, may reasonably make the world conclude, that either I can do nothing tolerably, or that this poem is not much amiss. Few good pictures have been finished at one sitting; neither can a true just play, which is to bear the test of ages, be produced at a heat, or by the force of fancy, without the maturity of judgment. For my own part, I have both so just a diffidence of myself, and so great a reverence for my audience, that I dare venture nothing without a strict examination; and am as much ashamed to put a loose indigested play upon the public, as I should be to offer brass money in a payment; for though it should be taken, (as it is too often on the stage) yet it would be found in the second telling; and a judicious reader will discover, in his closet, that trashy stuff, whose glittering deceived him in the action. I have often heard the stationer sighing in his shop, and wishing for those hands to take off his melancholy bargain, which clapped its performance on the stage. In a playhouse, every thing contributes to impose upon the judgment; the lights, the scenes, the habits, and, above all, the grace of action, which is commonly the best where there is the most need of it, surprise the audience, and cast a mist upon their understandings; not unlike the cunning of a juggler, who is always staring us in the face, and over-whelming us with gibberish, only that he may gain the opportunity of making the cleaner conveyance of his trick. But these false beauties of the stage are no more lasting than a rainbow; when the actor ceases to shine upon them, when he gilds them no longer with his reflection, they vanish in a twinkling. I have sometimes wondered, in the reading, what was become of those glaring colours which amazed me in "Bussy D'Amboys" upon the theatre; but when I had taken up what I supposed a fallen star, I found I had been cozened with a jelly[2]; nothing but a cold, dull mass, which glittered no longer than it was shooting; a dwarfish thought, dressed up in gigantic words, repetition in abundance, looseness of expression, and gross hyperboles; the sense of one line expanded prodigiously into ten; and, to sum up all, uncorrect English, and a hideous mingle of false poetry, and true nonsense; or, at best, a scantling of wit, which lay gasping for life, and groaning beneath a heap of rubbish. A famous modern poet used to sacrifice every year a Statius to Virgil's manes[3]; and I have indignation enough to burn a D'AMBOIS annually, to the memory of Jonson[4]. But now, my lord, I am sensible, perhaps too late, that I have gone too far: for, I remember some verses of my own Maximin and Almanzor, which cry vengeance upon me for their extravagance, and which I wish heartily in the same fire with Statius and Chapman. All I can say for those passages, which are, I hope, not many, is, that I knew they were bad enough to please, even when I wrote them; but I repent of them amongst my sins; and, if any of their fellows intrude by chance into my present writings, I draw a stroke over all those Dalilah's of the theatre; and am resolved I will settle myself no reputation by the applause of fools. It is not that I am mortified to all ambition, but I scorn as much to take it from half-witted judges, as I should to raise an estate by cheating of bubbles. Neither do I discommend the lofty style in tragedy, which is naturally pompous and magnificent; but nothing is truly sublime, that is not just and proper. If the antients had judged by the same measure, which a common reader takes, they had concluded Statius to have written higher than Virgil, for,

Quæ super-imposito moles geminata Colosso

carries a more thundering kind of sound, than

Tityre, tu patulæ recubans sub tegmine fagi:

yet Virgil had all the majesty of a lawful prince, and Statius only the blustering of a tyrant. But when men affect a virtue which they cannot easily reach, they fall into a vice, which bears the nearest resemblance to it. Thus, an injudicious poet, who aims at loftiness, runs easily into the swelling puffy style, because it looks like greatness. I remember, when I was a boy, I thought inimitable Spencer a mean poet, in comparison of Sylvester's "Dubartas," and was wrapt into an ecstasy when I read these lines:

Now, when the winter's keener breath began
To crystalize the Baltic ocean;
To glaze the lakes, to bridle up the floods,
And periwig with snow the bald-pate woods:—[5]

I am much deceived if this be not abominable fustian, that is, thoughts and words ill-sorted, and without the least relation to each other; yet I dare not answer for an audience, that they would not clap it on the stage: so little value there is to be given to the common cry, that nothing but madness can please madmen, and the poet must be of a piece with the spectators, to gain a reputation with them. But, as in a room, contrived for state, the height of the roof should bear a proportion to the area; so, in the heightenings of poetry, the strength and vehemence of figures should be suited to the occasion, the subject, and the persons. All beyond this is monstrous: it is out of nature, it is an excrescence, and not a living part of poetry. I had not said thus much, if some young gallants, who pretend to criticism, had not told me, that this tragi-comedy wanted the dignity of style; but, as a man, who is charged with a crime of which he thinks himself innocent, is apt to be too eager in his own defence; so, perhaps, I have vindicated my play with more partiality than I ought, or than such a trifle can deserve. Yet, whatever beauties it may want, it is free at least from the grossness of those faults I mentioned: what credit it has gained upon the stage, I value no farther than in reference to my profit, and the satisfaction I had, in seeing it represented with all the justness and gracefulness of action. But, as it is my interest to please my audience, so it is my ambition to be read: that I am sure is the more lasting and the nobler design: for the propriety of thoughts and words, which are the hidden beauties of a play, are but confusedly judged in the vehemence of action: all things are there beheld, as in a hasty motion, where the objects only glide before the eye, and disappear. The most discerning critic can judge no more of these silent graces in the action, than he who rides post through an unknown country can distinguish the situation of places, and the nature of the soil. The purity of phrase, the clearness of conception and expression, the boldness maintained to majesty, the significancy and sound of words, not strained into bombast, but justly elevated; in short, those very words and thoughts, which cannot be changed, but for the worse, must of necessity escape our transient view upon the theatre; and yet, without all these, a play may take. For, if either the story move us, or the actor help the lameness of it with his performance, or now and then a glittering beam of wit or passion strike through the obscurity of the poem, any of these are sufficient to effect a present liking, but not to fix a lasting admiration; for nothing but truth can long continue; and time is the surest judge of truth. I am not vain enough to think that I have left no faults in this, which that touchstone will not discover; neither, indeed, is it possible to avoid them in a play of this nature. There are evidently two actions in it; but it will be clear to any judicious man, that with half the pains I could have raised a play from either of them; but for this time I satisfied my humour, which was to tack two plays together; and to break a rule for the pleasure of variety. The truth is, the audience are grown weary of continued melancholy scenes; and I dare venture to prophecy, that few tragedies, except those in verse, shall succeed in this age, if they are not lightened with a course of mirth; for the feast is too dull and solemn without the fiddles. But how difficult a task this is, will soon be tried; for a several genius is required to either way; and, without both of them, a man, in my opinion, is but half a poet for the stage. Neither is it so trivial an undertaking, to make a tragedy end happily; for it is more difficult to save, than it is to kill. The dagger and the cup of poison are always in a readiness; but to bring the action to the last extremity, and then by probable means to recover all, will require the art and judgement of a writer; and cost him many a pang in the performance.

And now, my lord, I must confess, that what I have written, looks more like a Preface, than a Dedication; and, truly, it was thus far my design, that I might entertain you with somewhat in my own art, which might be more worthy of a noble mind, than the stale exploded trick of fulsome panegyrics. It is difficult to write justly on any thing, but almost impossible in praise. I shall therefore wave so nice a subject; and only tell you, that, in recommending a protestant play to a protestant patron, as I do myself an honour, so I do your noble family a right, who have been always eminent in the support and favour of our religion and liberties. And if the promises of your youth, your education at home, and your experience abroad, deceive me not, the principles you have embraced are such, as will no way degenerate from your ancestors, but refresh their memory in the minds of all true Englishmen, and renew their lustre in your person; which, my lord, is not more the wish, than it is the constant expectation, of

Your lordship's
Most obedient, faithful servant,
JOHN DRYDEN.

Footnotes

1. *John, Lord Haughton, eldest son of the Earl of Clare. succeeded to his father, was created Marquis of Clare, and died 1711, leaving an only daughter, who married the eldest son of the famous Robert Harley, Earl of Oxford.*

2. *See note on OEdipus, p. 151.*

3. *Dryden appears to have alluded to the following passage in Strada, though without a very accurate recollection of its contents: "Sane Andreas Naugerius Valerio Martiali acriter infensus, solemne jam habebat in illum aliquanto petulantius jocari. Etenim natali suo, accitis ad geniale epulum amicis, postquam prolixe de poeticæ laudibus super mensam disputaverat; ostensurum se aiebat a cæna, quo tandem modo laudari poesim deceret: Mox aferri jubebat Martialis volumen, (hæc erat mensæ appendix) atque igni proprior factus, illustri conflagratione absumendum flammis imponebat: addebatque eo incendio litare se Musis, Manibusque Virgilij, cujus imitatorem cultoremque prestare se*

melius haud posset, quam si vilia poetarum capita per undas insecutus ac flammas perpetuo perdidisset. Nec se eo loco tenuit, sed cum Silvas aliquot ab se conscriptas legisset, audissetque Statianu characteri similes videri, iratus sibi, quod a Martiale fugiens alio declinasset a Virgilio, cum primum se recessit domum, in Silvas conjecit ignem." Stradæ Prolusiones, Lib. II. Pro. 5. From this passage, it is obvious, that it was Martial, not Statius, whom Andreas Navagero sacrificed to Virgil, although he burned his own verses when they were accused of a resemblance to the style of the author of the Thebaid. In the same prolusion, Strada quotes the "blustering" line, afterwards censured by Dryden; but erroneously reads,

Super imposito moles gemmata colosso.

4. "Bussy D'Ambois," a tragedy, once much applauded, was the favourite production of George Chapman. If Dryden could have exhausted every copy of this bombast performance in one holocaust, the public would have been no great losers, as may be apparent from the following quotations:

Bussy. I'll sooth his plots, and strew my hate with smiles,
Till, all at once, the close mines of my heart
Rise at full state, and rush into his blood.
I'll bind his arm in silk, and rub his flesh,
To make the veine swell, that his soule may gush
Into some kennel, where it loves to lie;
And policy be flanked with policy.
Yet shall the feeling centre, where we meet.
Groan with the weight of my approaching feet.
I'll make the inspired threshold of his court
Sweat with the weather of my horrid steps,
Before I enter; yet, I will appear
Like calm securitie, befor a ruin.
A politician must, like lightning, melt
The very marrow, and not taint the skin;
His wayes must not be seen through, the superficies
Of the green centre must not taste his feet,
When hell is plowed up with the wounding tracts,
And all his harvest reap't by hellish facts.

Montsurry, when he discovers that the Friar had acted as confident in the intrigue betwixt his lady and d'Ambois, thus elegantly expresses the common idea of the world being turned upside down.

Now, is it true, earth moves, and heaven stands still;
Even heaven itself must see and suffer ill.
The too huge bias of the world hath swayed
Her back-part upwards, and with that she braves
This hemisphere, that long her month hath mocked.
The gravity of her religious face,
Now grown too weighty with her sacrilege,
And here discerned sophisticate enough,
Turns to the antipodes, and all the forms
That here allusions have impressed in her,
Have eaten through her back, and now all see

How she is riveted with hypocrisie.

Yet, I observe, from the prologue to the edition of 1641, that the part of D'Ambois was considered as a high test of a players' talents:

—Field is gone,
Whose action first did give it name; and one
Who came the neatest to him, is denied,
By his grey beard, to shew the height and pride
Of d'Ambois' youth and braverie. Yet to hold
Our title still a-foot, and not grow cold,
By giving't o'er, a third man with his best
Of care and paines defends our interest.
As Richard he was liked, nor do we fear,
In personating d'Ambois, heile appear
To faint, or goe lesse, so your free consent,
As heretofore, give him encouragement.

I believe the successor of Field, in this once favourite character, was Hart. The piece was revived after the Restoration with great success.

5. Dryden has elsewhere ridiculed this absurd passage. The original has "periwig with wool."

PROLOGUE

Now, luck for us, and a kind hearty pit;
For he, who pleases, never fails of wit:
Honour is yours;
And you, like kings at city-treats, bestow it;
The writer kneels, and is bid rise a poet;
But you are fickle sovereigns, to our sorrow;
You dub to-day, and hang a man to-morrow:
You cry the same sense up, and down again,
Just like brass-money once a year in Spain:
Take you in the mood, whate'er base metal come,
You coin as fast as groats at Birmingham:
Though 'tis no more like sense, in antient plays,
Than Rome's religion like St Peter's days.
In short, so swift your judgments turn and wind,
You cast our fleetest wits a mile behind.
'Twere well your judgments but in plays did range,
But e'en your follies and debauches change
With such a whirl, the poets of our age
Are tired, and cannot score them on the stage;
Unless each vice in short-hand they indict,
Even as notch'd prentices whole sermons write[1].

The heavy Hollanders no vices know,
But what they used a hundred years ago;
Like honest plants, where they were stuck, they grow.
They cheat, but still from cheating sires they come;
They drink, but they were christened first in mum.
Their patrimonial sloth the Spaniards keep,
And Philip first taught Philip how to sleep.
The French and we still change; but here's the curse,
They change for better, and we change for worse;
They take up our old trade of conquering,
And we are taking theirs, to dance and sing:
Our fathers did, for change, to France repair,
And they, for change, will try our English air;
As children, when they throw one toy away,
Strait a more foolish gewgaw comes in play:
So we, grown penitent, on serious thinking,
Leave whoring, and devoutly fall to drinking.
Scowering the watch grows out-of-fashion wit:
Now we set up for tilting in the pit,
Where 'tis agreed by bullies chicken-hearted,
To fright the ladies first, and then be parted.
A fair attempt has twice or thrice been made,
To hire night murderers, and make death a trade[2].
When murder's out, what vice can we advance?
Unless the new-found poisoning trick of France:
And, when their art of rats-bane we have got,
By way of thanks, we'll send them o'er our plot.

Footnotes

1. It was anciently a part of the apprentice's duty, not only to carry the family bible to church, but to take notes of the sermon for the edification of his master or mistress.

2. Alluding apparently to the assassination of Thomas Thynne, esq. in Pall-Mall, by the hired bravoes of count Coningsmark.

DRAMATIS PERSONÆ

TORRISMOND, Son of SANCHO, the deposed King, believing himself Son of RAYMOND.
BERTRAN, a Prince of the blood.
ALPHONSO, a general Officer, Brother to RAYMOND.
LORENZO, his Son.
RAYMOND, a Nobleman, supposed Father of TORRISMOND.
PEDRO, an Officer.
GOMEZ, an old Usurer.

DOMINICK, the Spanish Friar.

LEONORA, Queen of Arragon.
TERESA, Woman to LEONORA.
ELVIRA, Wife to GOMEZ.

THE SPANISH FRIAR

Or, THE DOUBLE DISCOVERY

ACT I

SCENE I

ALPHONSO and **PEDRO** meet, with **SOLDIERS** on each Side, Drums, &c.

ALPHONSO
Stand: give the word.

PEDRO
The queen of Arragon.

ALPHONSO
Pedro?—how goes the night?

PEDRO
She wears apace.

ALPHONSO
Then welcome day-light; we shall have warm work on't.
The Moor will 'gage
His utmost forces on this next assault,
To win a queen and kingdom.

PEDRO
Pox on this lion-way of wooing, though.
Is the queen stirring yet?

ALPHONSO
She has not been abed, but in her chapel
All night devoutly watched, and bribed the saints
With vows for her deliverance.

PEDRO
O, Alphonso!
I fear they come too late. Her father's crimes

Sit heavy on her, and weigh down her prayers.
A crown usurped; a lawful king deposed,
In bondage held, debarred the common light;
His children murdered, and his friends destroyed,—
What can we less expect than what we feel,
And what we fear will follow?

ALPHONSO
Heaven avert it!

PEDRO
Then heaven must not be heaven. Judge the event
By what has passed. The usurper joyed not long
His ill-got crown:—'tis true, he died in peace,—
Unriddle that, ye powers!—but left his daughter,
Our present queen, engaged upon his death-bed,
To marry with young Bertran, whose cursed father
Had helped to make him great.
Hence, you well know, this fatal war arose;
Because the Moor Abdalla, with whose troops
The usurper gained the kingdom, was refused;
And, as an infidel, his love despised.

ALPHONSO
Well, we are soldiers, Pedro; and, like lawyers,
Plead for our pay.

PEDRO
A good cause would do well though:
It gives my sword an edge. You see this Bertran
Has now three times been beaten by the Moors:
What hope we have, is in young Torrismond,
Your brother's son.

ALPHONSO
He's a successful warrior,
And has the soldiers' hearts: upon the skirts
Of Arragon our squandered troops he rallies.
Our watchmen from the towers with longing eyes
Expect his swift arrival.

PEDRO
It must be swift, or it will come too late.

ALPHONSO
No more.—Duke Bertran.

[Enter **BERTRAN** attended.

BERTRAN
Relieve the sentries that have watched all night.
[To **PEDRO**] Now, colonel, have you disposed your men,
That you stand idle here?

PEDRO
Mine are drawn off
To take a short repose.

BERTRAN
Short let it be:
For, from the Moorish camp, this hour and more,
There has been heard a distant humming noise,
Like bees disturbed, and arming in their hives.
What courage in our soldiers? Speak! What hope?

PEDRO
As much as when physicians shake their heads,
And bid their dying patient think of heaven.
Our walls are thinly manned; our best men slain;
The rest, an heartless number, spent with watching,
And harassed out with duty.

BERTRAN
Good-night all, then.

PEDRO
Nay, for my part, 'tis but a single life
I have to lose. I'll plant my colours down
In the mid-breach, and by them fix my foot;
Say a short soldier's prayer, to spare the trouble
Of my new friends above; and then expect
The next fair bullet.

ALPHONSO
Never was known a night of such distraction;
Noise so confused and dreadful; jostling crowds,
That run, and know not whither; torches gliding,
Like meteors, by each other in the streets.

PEDRO
I met a reverend, fat, old gouty friar,—
With a paunch swoll'n so high, his double chin
Might rest upon it; a true son of the church;
Fresh-coloured, well thriven on his trade,—
Come puffing with his greasy bald-pate choir,
And fumbling o'er his beads in such an agony,

He told them false, for fear. About his neck
There hung a wench, the label of his function,
Whom he shook off, i'faith, methought, unkindly.
It seems the holy stallion durst not score
Another sin, before he left the world.

[Enter a **CAPTAIN**.

CAPTAIN
To arms, my lord, to arms!
From the Moors' camp the noise grows louder still:
Rattling of armour, trumpets, drums, and ataballes;
And sometimes peals of shouts that rend the heavens,
Like victory: then groans again, and howlings,
Like those of vanquished men; but every echo
Goes fainter off, and dies in distant sounds.

BERTRAN
Some false attack: expect on t'other side.
One to the gunners on St Jago's tower; bid them, for shame,
Level their cannon lower: On my soul
They are all corrupted with the gold of Barbary,
To carry over, and not hurt the Moor.

[Enter a **SECOND CAPTAIN**.

2ND CAPTAIN
My lord, here's fresh intelligence arrived.
Our army, led by valiant Torrismond,
Is now in hot engagement with the Moors;
'Tis said, within their trenches.

BERTRAN
I think all fortune is reserved for him!—
He might have sent us word though;
And then we could have favoured his attempt
With sallies from the town.

ALPHONSO
It could not be:
We were so close blocked up, that none could peep
Upon the walls and live. But yet 'tis time.

BERTRAN
No, 'tis too late; I will not hazard it:
On pain of death, let no man dare to sally.

PEDRO

Oh envy, envy, how it works within him! [Aside.
How now? what means this show?

ALPHONSO
'Tis a procession.
The queen is going to the great cathedral,
To pray for our success against the Moors.

PEDRO
Very good: she usurps the throne, keeps the old king in prison, and, at the same time, is praying for a blessing. Oh religion and roguery, how they go together!

[A Procession of **PRIESTS** and **CHORISTERS** in White, with Tapers, followed by the **QUEEN** and **LADIES**, goes over the Stage: the Choristers singing,

Look down, ye blessed above, look down,
Behold our weeping matrons' tears,
Behold our tender virgins' fears,
And with success our armies crown.

Look down, ye blessed above, look down:
Oh! save us, save as, and our state restore;
For pity, pity, pity, we implore:
For pity, pity, pity, we implore.

[The **PROCESSION** goes off; and shout within. Then

[Enter **LORENZO**, who kneels to **ALPHONSO**.

BERTRAN [To **ALPHONSO**]
A joyful cry; and see your son
Lorenzo. Good news, kind heaven!

ALPHONSO [To **LORENZO**]
O welcome, welcome! is the general safe?
How near our army? when shall we be succoured?
Or, are we succoured? are the Moors removed?
Answer these questions first, and then a thousand more;
Answer them all together.

LORENZO
Yes, when I have a thousand tongues, I will.
The general's well; his army too is safe,
As victory can make them. The Moors' king
Is safe enough, I warrant him, for one.
At dawn of day our general cleft his pate,
Spite of his woollen night-cap: a slight wound;
Perhaps he may recover.

ALPHONSO
Thou reviv'st me.

PEDRO
By my computation now, the victory was gained before the procession was made for it; and yet it will go hard but the priests will make a miracle of it.

LORENZO
Yes, faith; we came like bold intruding guests,
And took them unprepared to give us welcome.
Their scouts we killed, then found their body sleeping;
And as they lay confused, we stumbled o'er them,
And took what joint came next, arms, heads, or legs,
Somewhat indecently. But when men want light,
They make but bungling work.

BERTRAN
I'll to the queen,
And bear the news.

PEDRO
That's young Lorenzo's duty.

BERTRAN
I'll spare his trouble.—
This Torrismond begins to grow too fast;
He must be mine, or ruined.

[Aside, and Exit.

LORENZO
Pedro a word:—[whisper.]

ALPHONSO
How swift he shot away! I find it stung him,
In spite of his dissembling.
[To **LORENZO**] How many of the enemy are slain?

LORENZO
Troth, sir, we were in haste, and could not stay
To score the men we killed; but there they lie:
Best send our women out to take the tale;
There's circumcision in abundance for them.

[Turns to **PEDRO** again.

ALPHONSO

How far did you pursue them?

LORENZO
Some few miles.—
[To **PEDRO**] Good store of harlots, say you, and dog-cheap?
Pedro, they must be had, and speedily;
I've kept a tedious fast. [Whisper again.

ALPHONSO
When will he make his entry? he deserves
Such triumphs as were given by ancient Rome:
Ha, boy, what say'st thou?

LORENZO
As you say, sir, that Rome was very ancient.
[To **PEDRO**] I leave the choice to you; fair, black, tall, low,
Let her but have a nose; and you may tell her,
I am rich in jewels, rings, and bobbing pearls,
Plucked from Moors' ears.

ALPHONSO
Lorenzo.

LORENZO
Somewhat busy
About affairs relating to the public.—
A seasonable girl, just in the nick now—[To **PEDRO**.

[Trumpets within.

PEDRO
I hear the general's trumpet. Stand and mark
How he will be received; I fear, but coldly.
There hung a cloud, methought, on Bertran's brow.

LORENZO
Then look to see a storm on Torrismond's;
Looks fright not men. The general has seen Moors
With as bad faces; no dispraise to Bertran's.

PEDRO
'Twas rumoured in the camp, he loves the queen.

LORENZO
He drinks her health devoutly.

ALPHONSO
That may breed bad blood betwixt him and Bertran.

PEDRO
Yes, in private.
But Bertran has been taught the arts of court,
To gild a face with smiles, and leer a man to ruin,
O here they come.—

[Enter **TORRISMOND** and **OFFICERS** on one Side, **BERTRAN** attended on the other; they embrace, **BERTRAN** bowing low.

Just as I prophesied.—

LORENZO
Death and hell, he laughs at him!—in his face too.

PEDRO
O you mistake him; 'twas an humble grin,
The fawning joy of courtiers and of dogs.

LORENZO
Here are nothing but lies to be expected: I'll even go lose myself in some blind alley, and try if any courteous damsel will think me worth the finding.

[Aside, and Exit.

ALPHONSO
Now he begins to open.

BERTRAN
Your country rescued, and your queen relieved,—
A glorious conquest, noble Torrismond!
The people rend the skies with loud applause,
And heaven can hear no other name but yours.
The thronging crowds press on you as you pass,
And with their eager joy make triumph slow.

TORRISMOND
My lord, I have no taste
Of popular applause; the noisy praise
Of giddy crowds, as changeable as winds;
Still vehement, and still without a cause;
Servant to chance, and blowing in the tide
Of swoln success; but veering with its ebb,
It leaves the channel dry.

BERTRAN
So young a stoick!

TORRISMOND
You wrong me, if you think I'll sell one drop
Within these veins for pageants; but, let honour
Call for my blood, and sluice it into streams:
Turn fortune loose again to my pursuit,
And let me hunt her through embattled foes,
In dusty plains, amidst the cannons' roar,
There will I be the first.

BERTRAN
I'll try him farther.—[Aside.
Suppose the assembled states of Arragon
Decree a statue to you, thus inscribed:
"To Torrismond, who freed his native land."

ALPHONSO [To **PEDRO**]
Mark how he sounds and fathoms him,
To find the shallows of his soul!

BERTRAN
The just applause
Of god-like senates, is the stamp of virtue,
Which makes it pass unquestioned through the world.
These honours you deserve; nor shall my suffrage
Be last to fix them on you. If refused,
You brand us all with black ingratitude:
For times to come shall say,—Our Spain, like Rome,
Neglects her champions after noble acts,
And lets their laurels wither on their heads.

TORRISMOND
A statue, for a battle blindly fought,
Where darkness and surprise made conquest cheap!
Where virtue borrowed but the arms of chance,
And struck a random blow!—'Twas fortune's work,
And fortune take the praise.

BERTRAN
Yet happiness
Is the first fame. Virtue without success
Is a fair picture shewn by an ill light;
But lucky men are favourites of heaven:
And whom should kings esteem above heaven's darlings?
The praises of a young and beauteous queen
Shall crown your glorious acts.

PEDRO [To **ALPHONSO**]
There sprung the mine.

TORRISMOND
The queen! that were a happiness too great!
Named you the queen, my lord?

BERTRAN
Yes: you have seen her, and you must confess,
A praise, a smile, a look from her is worth
The shouts of thousand amphitheatres.
She, she shall praise you, for I can oblige her:
To-morrow will deliver all her charms
Into my arms, and make her mine for ever.—
Why stand you mute?

TORRISMOND
Alas! I cannot speak.

BERTRAN
Not speak, my lord! How were your thoughts employed?

TORRISMOND
Nor can I think, or I am lost in thought.

BERTRAN
Thought of the queen, perhaps?

TORRISMOND
Why, if it were,
Heaven may be thought on, though too high to climb.

BERTRAN
O, now I find where your ambition drives!
You ought not to think of her.

TORRISMOND
So I say too,
I ought not; madmen ought not to be mad;
But who can help his frenzy?

BERTRAN
Fond young man!
The wings of your ambition must be clipt:
Your shame-faced virtue shunned the people's praise,
And senate's honours: But 'tis well we know
What price you hold yourself at. You have fought
With some success, and that has sealed your pardon.

TORRISMOND

Pardon from thee!—O, give me patience, heaven!—
Thrice vanquished Bertran, if thou dar'st, look out
Upon yon slaughtered host, that field of blood;
There seal my pardon, where thy fame was lost.

PEDRO
He's ruined, past redemption!

ALPHONSO [To **TORRISMOND**]
Learn respect
To the first prince of the blood.

BERTRAN
O, let him rave!
I'll not contend with madmen.

TORRISMOND
I have done:
I know, 'twas madness to declare this truth:
And yet, 'twere baseness to deny my love.
'Tis true, my hopes are vanishing as clouds;
Lighter than children's bubbles blown by winds:
My merit's but the rash result of chance;
My birth unequal; all the stars against me:
Power, promise, choice, the living and the dead;
Mankind my foes; and only love to friend:
But such a love, kept at such awful distance,
As, what it loudly dares to tell a rival,
Shall fear to whisper there. Queens may be loved,
And so may gods; else why are altars raised?
Why shines the sun, but that he may be viewed?
But, oh! when he's too bright, if then we gaze,
'Tis but to weep, and close our eyes in darkness.

[Exit.

BERTRAN
'Tis well; the goddess shall be told, she shall,
Of her new worshipper.

[Exit.

PEDRO
So, here's fine work!
He has supplied his only foe with arms
For his destruction. Old Penelope's tale
Inverted; he has unravelled all by day,
That he has done by night. What, planet struck!

ALPHONSO
I wish I were; to be past sense of this!

PEDRO
Would I had but a lease of life so long,
As 'till my flesh and blood rebelled this way,
Against our sovereign lady;—mad for a queen?
With a globe in one hand, and a sceptre in t'other?
A very pretty moppet!

ALPHONSO
Then to declare his madness to his rival!
His father absent on an embassy;
Himself a stranger almost; wholly friendless!
A torrent, rolling down a precipice,
Is easier to be stopt, than is his ruin.

PEDRO
'Tis fruitless to complain; haste to the court;
Improve your interest there for pardon from the queen.

ALPHONSO
Weak remedies;
But all must be attempted.

[Exit.

SCENE II

Enter **LORENZO**.

LORENZO
Well, I am the most unlucky rogue! I have been ranging over half the town; but have sprung no game. Our women are worse infidels than the Moors: I told them I was one of the knight-errants, that delivered them from ravishment; and I think in my conscience, that is their quarrel to me.

PEDRO
Is this a time for fooling? Your cousin is run honourably mad in love with her majesty; he is split upon a rock, and you, who are in chase of harlots, are sinking in the main ocean. I think, the devil's in the family.

[Exit.

LORENZO [Solus.]

My cousin ruined, says he! hum, not that I wish my kinsman's ruin; that were unchristian: but, if the general is ruined, I am heir; there's comfort for a Christian! Money I have; I thank the honest Moors for it; but I want a mistress. I am willing to be lewd; but the tempter is wanting on his part.

[Enter **ELVIRA**, veiled.

ELVIRA
Stranger! Cavalier!—will you not hear me? you Moor-killer, you
Matador!—

LORENZO
Meaning me, madam?

ELVIRA
Face about, man! you a soldier, and afraid of the enemy!

LORENZO
I must confess, I did not expect to have been charged first: I see souls will not be lost for want of diligence in this devil's reign. [Aside.] Now, Madam Cynthia, behind a cloud, your will and pleasure with me?

ELVIRA
You have the appearance of a cavalier; and if you are as deserving as you seem, perhaps you may not repent of your adventure. If a lady like you well enough to hold discourse with you at first sight; you are gentleman enough, I hope, to help her out with an apology, and to lay the blame on stars, or destiny, or what you please, to excuse the frailty of a woman?

LORENZO
O, I love an easy woman! there's such ado, to crack a thick-shelled mistress; we break our teeth, and find no kernel. 'Tis generous in you, to take pity on a stranger, and not to suffer him to fall into ill hands at his first arrival.

ELVIRA
You may have a better opinion of me than I deserve; you have not seen me yet; and, therefore, I am confident you are heart-whole.

LORENZO
Not absolutely slain, I must confess; but I am drawing on apace: you have a dangerous tongue in your head, I can tell you that; and if your eyes prove of as killing metal, there is but one way with me. Let me see you, for the safeguard of my honour; 'tis but decent the cannon should be drawn down upon me before I yield.

ELVIRA
What a terrible similitude have you made, colonel, to shew that you are inclining to the wars? I could answer you with another in my profession: Suppose you were in want of money, would you not be glad to take a sum upon content in a sealed bag, without peeping?—but, however, I will not stand with you for a sample.

[Lifts up her veil.

LORENZO
What eyes were there! how keen their glances! you do well to keep them veiled; they are too sharp to be trusted out of the scabbard.

ELVIRA
Perhaps now, you may accuse my forwardness; but this day of jubilee is the only time of freedom I have had; and there is nothing so extravagant as a prisoner, when he gets loose a little, and is immediately to return into his fetters.

LORENZO
To confess freely to you, madam, I was never in love with less than your whole sex before; but now I have seen you, I am in the direct road of languishing and sighing; and, if love goes on as it begins, for aught I know, by to-morrow morning you may hear of me in rhyme and sonnet. I tell you truly, I do not like these symptoms in myself. Perhaps I may go shufflingly at first; for I was never before walked in trammels; yet, I shall drudge and moil at constancy, till I have worn off the hitching in my pace.

ELVIRA
Oh, sir, there are arts to reclaim the wildest men, as there are to make spaniels fetch and carry: chide them often, and feed them seldom. Now I know your temper, you may thank yourself, if you are kept to hard meat. You are in for years, if you make love to me.

LORENZO
I hate a formal obligation with an Anno Domini at end on't; there may be an evil meaning in the word years, called matrimony.

ELVIRA
I can easily rid you of that fear: I wish I could rid myself as easily of the bondage.

LORENZO
Then you are married?

ELVIRA
If a covetous, and a jealous, and an old man be a husband.

LORENZO
Three as good qualities for my purpose as I could wish: now love be praised!

[Enter **ELVIRA'S DUENNA**, and whispers to her.

ELVIRA [Aside.]
If I get not home before my husband, I shall be ruined. [To him.] I dare not stay to tell you where. Farewell!—Could I once more—

[Exit.

LORENZO

This is unconscionable dealing; to be made a slave, and know not whose livery I wear. Who have we yonder?

[Enter **GOMEZ**.

By that shambling in his walk, it should be my rich old banker, Gomez, whom I knew at Barcelona: As I live 'tis he!—What, old Mammon here!
[To **GOMEZ**.

GOMEZ
How! young Beelzebub?

LORENZO
What devil has set his claws in thy haunches, and brought thee hither to Saragossa? Sure he meant a farther journey with thee.

GOMEZ
I always remove before the enemy: When the Moors are ready to besiege one town, I shift quarters to the next; I keep as far from the infidels as I can.

LORENZO
That's but a hair's breadth at farthest.

GOMEZ
Well, you have got a famous victory; all true subjects are overjoyed at it: There are bonfires decreed; an the times had not been hard, my billet should have burnt too.

LORENZO
I dare say for thee, thou hast such a respect for a single billet, thou wouldst almost have thrown on thyself to save it; thou art for saving every thing but thy soul.

GOMEZ
Well, well, you'll not believe me generous, 'till I carry you to the tavern, and crack half a pint with you at my own charges.

LORENZO
No; I'll keep thee from hanging thyself for such an extravagance; and, instead of it, thou shalt do me a mere verbal courtesy. I have just now seen a most incomparable young lady.

GOMEZ
Whereabouts did you see this most incomparable young lady?—My mind misgives me plaguily. [Aside.

LORENZO
Here, man, just before this corner-house: Pray heaven, it prove no bawdy-house.

GOMEZ [Aside.]
Pray heaven, he does not make it one!

LORENZO
What dost thou mutter to thyself? Hast thou any thing to say against the honesty of that house?

GOMEZ
Not I, colonel; the walls are very honest stone, and the timber very honest wood, for aught I know; but for the woman, I cannot say, till I know her better: Describe her person, and, if she live in this quarter, I may give you tidings of her.

LORENZO
She is of a middle stature, dark-coloured hair, the most bewitching leer with her eyes, the most roguish cast! her cheeks are dimpled when she smiles, and her smiles would tempt an hermit.

GOMEZ [Aside.]
I am dead, I am buried, I am damned.—Go on, colonel; have you no other marks of her?

LORENZO
Thou hast all her marks; but she has a husband, a jealous, covetous, old hunks: Speak! canst thou tell me news of her?

GOMEZ
Yes; this news, colonel, that you have seen your last of her.

LORENZO
If thou help'st me not to the knowledge of her, thou art a circumcised Jew.

GOMEZ
Circumcise me no more than I circumcise you, colonel Hernando:
Once more, you have seen your last of her.

LORENZO [Aside.]
I am glad he knows me only by that name of Hernando, by which I went at Barcelona; now he can tell no tales of me to my father.—[To him.] Come, thou wer't ever good-natured, when thou couldst get by it—Look here, rogue; 'tis of the right damning colour: Thou art not proof against gold, sure!—Do not I know thee for a covetous—

GOMEZ
Jealous old hunks? those were the marks of your mistress's husband, as I remember, colonel.

LORENZO
Oh the devil! What a rogue in understanding was I, not to find him out sooner! [Aside.

GOMEZ
Do, do, look sillily, good colonel; 'tis a decent melancholy after an absolute defeat.

LORENZO
Faith, not for that, clear Gomez; but—

GOMEZ

But—no pumping, my dear colonel.

LORENZO
Hang pumping! I was thinking a little upon a point of gratitude. We two have been long acquaintance; I know thy merits, and can make some interest;—Go to; thou wert born to authority; I'll make thee Alcaide, Mayor of Saragossa.

GOMEZ
Satisfy yourself; you shall not make me what you think, colonel.

LORENZO
Faith, but I will; thou hast the face of a magistrate already.

GOMEZ
And you would provide me with a magistrate's head to my magistrate's face; I thank you, colonel.

LORENZO
Come, thou art so suspicious upon an idle story! That woman I saw, I mean that little, crooked, ugly woman,—for t'other was a lie,—is no more thy wife,—As I'll go home with thee, and satisfy thee immediately, my dear friend.

GOMEZ
I shall not put you to that trouble; no, not so much as a single visit; not so much as an embassy by a civil old woman, nor a serenade of twinkledum twinkledum under my windows; nay, I will advise you, out of my tenderness to your person, that you walk not near yon corner-house by night; for, to my certain knowledge, there are blunderbusses planted in every loop-hole, that go off constantly of their own accord, at the squeaking of a fiddle, and the thrumming of a guitar.

LORENZO
Art thou so obstinate? Then I denounce open war against thee; I'll demolish thy citadel by force; or, at least, I'll bring my whole regiment upon thee; my thousand red locusts, that shall devour thee in free quarters. Farewell, wrought night-cap.

[Exit **LORENZO**.

GOMEZ
Farewell, Buff. Free quarters for a regiment of red-coat locusts? I hope to see them all in the Red-Sea first! But oh, this Jezabel of mine! I'll get a physician that shall prescribe her an ounce of camphire every morning, for her breakfast, to abate incontinency. She shall never peep abroad, no, not to church for confession; and, for never going, she shall be condemned for a heretic. She shall have stripes by Troy weight, and sustenance by drachms and scruples: Nay, I'll have a fasting almanack, printed on purpose for her use, in which
No Carnival nor Christmas shall appear,
But lents and ember-weeks shall fill the year.

[Exit.

ACT II

SCENE I.—The Queen's Antechamber

Enter **ALPHONSO** and **PEDRO**.

ALPHONSO
When saw you my Lorenzo?

PEDRO
I had a glimpse of him; but he shot by me,
Like a young hound upon a burning scent;
He's gone a harlot-hunting.

ALPHONSO
His foreign breeding might have taught him better.

PEDRO
'Tis that has taught him this.
What learn our youth abroad, but to refine
The homely vices of their native land?
Give me an honest home-spun country clown
Of our own growth; his dulness is but plain,
But theirs embroidered; they are sent out fools,
But come back fops.

ALPHONSO
You know what reasons urged me;
But now, I have accomplished my designs,
I should be glad he knew them. His wild riots
Disturb my soul; but they would sit more close,
Did not the threatened downfal of our house,
In Torrismond, o'erwhelm my private ills.

[Enter **BERTRAN**, attended, and whispering with a Courtier, aside.

BERTRAN
I would not have her think, he dared to love her;
If he presume to own it, she's so proud,
He tempts his certain ruin.

ALPHONSO [To **PEDRO**]
Mark how disdainfully he throws his eyes on us.
Our old imprisoned king wore no such looks.

PEDRO
O! would the general shake off his dotage to the usurping queen,

And re-enthrone good venerable Sancho,
I'll undertake, should Bertran sound his trumpets,
And Torrismond but whistle through his fingers,
He draws his army off.

ALPHONSO
I told him so;
But had an answer louder than a storm.

PEDRO
Now, plague and pox on his smock-loyalty!
I hate to see a brave bold fellow sotted,
Made sour and senseless, turned to whey by love;
A drivelling hero, fit for a romance.—
O, here he comes! what will their greetings be?

[Enter **TORRISMOND**, attended; **BERTRAN** and he meet and jostle.

BERTRAN
Make way, my lords, and let the pageant pass.

TORRISMOND
I make my way, where'er I see my foe;
But you, my lord, are good at a retreat.
I have no Moors behind me.

BERTRAN
Death and hell!
Dare to speak thus when you come out again.

TORRISMOND
Dare to provoke me thus, insulting man!

[Enter **TERESA**.

TERESA
My lords, you are too loud so near the queen;
You, Torrismond, have much offended her.
'Tis her command you instantly appear,
To answer your demeanour to the prince.

[Exit **TERESA; BERTRAN**, with his company, follow her.

TORRISMOND
O, Pedro, O, Alphonso, pity me!
A grove of pikes,
Whose polished steel from far severely shines,
Are not so dreadful as this beauteous queen.

ALPHONSO
Call up your courage timely to your aid,
And, like a lion, pressed upon the toils,
Leap on your hunters. Speak your actions boldly;
There is a time when modest virtue is
Allowed to praise itself.

PEDRO
Heart! you were hot enough, too hot, but now;
Your fury then boiled upward to a foam;
But since this message came, you sink and settle,
As if cold water had been poured upon you.

TORRISMOND
Alas! thou know'st not what it is to love!
When we behold an angel, not to fear,
Is to be impudent: No, I am resolved,
Like a led victim, to my death I'll go,
And, dying, bless the hand, that gave the blow.

[Exeunt.

The SCENE draws, and shews the **QUEEN** sitting in state; **BERTRAN** standing next to her; then **TERESA**, &c. She rises, and comes to the front.

LEONORA [To **BERTRAN**]
I blame not you, my lord; my father's will,
Your own deserts, and all my people's voice,
Have placed you in the view of sovereign power.
But I would learn the cause, why Torrismond,
Within my palace-walls, within my hearing,
Almost within my sight,—affronts a prince,
Who shortly shall command him.

BERTRAN
He thinks you owe him more than you can pay;
And looks as he were lord of human kind.

[Enter **TORRISMOND, ALPHONSO, PEDRO. TORRISMOND** bows low, then looks earnestly on the **QUEEN**, and keeps at Distance.

TERESA
Madam, the general.—

LEONORA
Let me view him well.
My father sent him early to the frontiers;

I have not often seen him; if I did,
He passed unmarked by my unheeding eyes:—
But where's the fierceness, the disdainful pride,
The haughty port, the fiery arrogance?—
By all these marks, this is not, sure, the man.

BERTRAN
Yet this is he, who filled your court with tumult,
Whose fierce demeanour, and whose insolence,
The patience of a god could not support.

LEONORA
Name his offence, my lord, and he shall have
Immediate punishment.

BERTRAN
'Tis of so high a nature, should I speak it,
That my presumption then would equal his.

LEONORA
Some one among you speak.

PEDRO
Now my tongue itches. [Aside.

LEONORA
All dumb! On your allegiance, Torrismond,
By all your hopes, I do command you, speak.

TORRISMOND [Kneeling.]
O seek not to convince me of a crime,
Which I can ne'er repent, nor can you pardon;
Or, if you needs will know it, think, oh think,
That he who, thus commanded, dares to speak,
Unless commanded, would have died in silence.
But you adjured me, madam, by my hopes!
Hopes I have none, for I am all despair;
Friends I have none, for friendship follows favour;
Desert I've none, for what I did was duty:—
Oh that it were!—that it were duty all!

LEONORA
Why do you pause? proceed.

TORRISMOND
As one, condemned to leap a precipice,
Who sees before his eyes the depth below,
Stops short, and looks about for some kind shrub

To break his dreadful fall.—so I—
But whither am I going? If to death,
He looks so lovely sweet in beauty's pomp,
He draws me to his dart.—I dare no more.

BERTRAN
He's mad, beyond the cure of hellebore.
Whips, darkness, dungeons, for this insolence.

TORRISMOND
Mad as I am, yet I know when to bear.

LEONORA
You're both too bold.—You, Torrismond, withdraw,
I'll teach you all what's owing to your queen.—
For you, my lord,—
The priest to-morrow was to join our hands;
I'll try if I can live a day without you.—
So both of you depart, and live in peace.

ALPHONSO
Who knows which way she points?
Doubling and turning like an hunted hare;—
Find out the meaning of her mind who can.

PEDRO
Who ever found a woman's? backward and forward,
The whole sex in every word.
In my conscience, when she was getting, her mother was thinking of a riddle.

[Exeunt all but the **QUEEN** and **TERESA**.

LEONORA
Haste, my Teresa, haste, and call him back.

TERESA
Whom, madam?

LEONORA
Him.

TERESA
Prince Bertran?

LEONORA
Torrismond;
There is no other he.

TERESA [Aside.]
A rising sun,
Or I am much deceived.

[Exit **TERESA**.

LEONORA
A change so swift what heart did ever feel!
It rushed upon me like a mighty stream,
And bore me, in a moment, far from shore.
I loved away myself; in one short hour
Already am I gone an age of passion.
Was it his youth, his valour, or success?
These might, perhaps, be found in other men:
'Twas that respect, that awful homage, paid me;
That fearful love, which trembled in his eyes,
And with a silent earthquake shook his soul.
But, when he spoke, what tender words he said!
So softly, that, like flakes of feathered snow,
They melted as they fell.—

[Enter **TERESA** with **TORRISMOND**.

TERESA
He waits your pleasure.

LEONORA
'Tis well; retire.—Oh heavens, that I must speak
So distant from my heart!— [Aside.
[To **TORRISMOND**] How now! What boldness brings you back again?

TORRISMOND
I heard 'twas your command.

LEONORA
A fond mistake,
To credit so unlikely a command;
And you return, full of the same presumption,
To affront me with your love!

TORRISMOND
If 'tis presumption, for a wretch condemned,
To throw himself beneath his judge's feet:
A boldness more than this I never knew;
Or, if I did, 'twas only to your foes.

LEONORA
You would insinuate your past services,

And those, I grant, were great; but you confess
A fault committed since, that cancels all.

TORRISMOND
And who could dare to disavow his crime,
When that, for which he is accused and seized,
He bears about him still! My eyes confess it;
My every action speaks my heart aloud:
But, oh, the madness of my high attempt
Speaks louder yet! and all together cry,—
I love and I despair.

LEONORA
Have you not heard,
My father, with his dying voice, bequeathed
My crown and me to Bertran? And dare you,
A private man, presume to love a queen?

TORRISMOND
That, that's the wound! I see you set so high,
As no desert or services can reach.—
Good heavens, why gave you me a monarch's soul,
And crusted it with base plebeian clay?
Why gave you me desires of such extent,
And such a span to grasp them? Sure, my lot
By some o'er-hasty angel was misplaced
In fate's eternal volume!—But I rave,
And, like a giddy bird in dead of night,
Fly round the fire that scorches me to death.

LEONORA
Yet, Torrismond, you've not so ill deserved,
But I may give you counsel for your cure.

TORRISMOND
I cannot, nay, I wish not to be cured.

LEONORA [Aside.]
Nor I, heaven knows!

TORRISMOND
There is a pleasure, sure,
In being mad, which none but madmen know!
Let me indulge it; let me gaze for ever!
And, since you are too great to be beloved,
Be greater, greater yet, and be adored.

LEONORA

These are the words which I must only hear
From Bertran's mouth; they should displease from you:
I say they should; but women are so vain,
To like the love, though they despise the lover.
Yet, that I may not send you from my sight
In absolute despair,—I pity you.

TORRISMOND
Am I then pitied! I have lived enough!—
Death, take me in this moment of my joy;
But, when my soul is plunged in long oblivion,
Spare this one thought! let me remember pity,
And, so deceived, think all my life was blessed.

LEONORA
What if I add a little to my alms?
If that would help, I could cast in a tear
To your misfortunes.

TORRISMOND
A tear! You have o'erbid all my past sufferings,
And all my future too!

LEONORA
Were I no queen—
Or you of royal blood—

TORRISMOND
What have I lost by my forefathers' fault!
Why was not I the twentieth by descent
From a long restive race of droning kings?
Love! what a poor omnipotence hast thou,
When gold and titles buy thee?

LEONORA [Sighs.]
Oh, my torture!—

TORRISMOND
Might I presume,—but, oh, I dare not hope
That sigh was added to your alms for me!

LEONORA
I give you leave to guess, and not forbid you
To make the best construction for your love:
Be secret and discreet; these fairy favours
Are lost, when not concealed[1].—provoke not Bertran.—
Retire: I must no more but this,—Hope, Torrismond.

[Exit.

TORRISMOND
She bids me hope; oh heavens, she pities me!
And pity still foreruns approaching love,
As lightning does the thunder! Tune your harps,
Ye angels, to that sound; and thou, my heart,
Make room to entertain thy flowing joy.
Hence, all my griefs and every anxious care;
One word, and one kind glance, can cure despair.

[Exit.

SCENE II—A Chamber. A Table and Wine Set Out

Enter **LORENZO**.

LORENZO
This may hit; 'tis more than barely possible; for friars have free admittance into every house. This jacobin, whom I have sent to, is her confessor; and who can suspect a man of such reverence for a pimp? I'll try for once; I'll bribe him high; for commonly none love money better than they, who have made a vow of poverty.

[Enter **SERVANT**.

SERVANT
There's a huge, fat, religious gentleman coming up, sir. He says he's but a friar, but he's big enough to be a pope; his gills are as rosy as a turkey cock's; his great belly walks in state before him, like an harbinger; and his gouty legs come limping after it: Never was such a ton of devotion seen.

LORENZO
Bring him in, and vanish.

[Exit **SERVANT**.

[Enter **Father DOMINICK**.

LORENZO
Welcome, father.

Father DOMINICK
Peace be here: I thought I had been sent for to a dying man; to have fitted him for another world.

LORENZO
No, faith, father, I was never for taking such long journeys. Repose yourself, I beseech you, sir, if those spindle legs of yours will carry you to the next chair.

Father DOMINICK
I am old, I am infirm, I must confess, with fasting.

LORENZO
'Tis a sign by your wan complexion, and your thin jowls, father. Come, to our better acquaintance:—here's a sovereign remedy for old age and sorrow.

[Drinks.

Father DOMINICK
The looks of it are indeed alluring: I'll do you reason.

[Drinks.

LORENZO
Is it to your palate, father?

Father DOMINICK
Second thoughts, they say, are best: I'll consider of it once again.

[Drinks.]

It has a most delicious flavour with it. Gad forgive me, I have forgotten to drink your health, Son, I am not used to be so unmannerly.

[Drinks again.

LORENZO
No, I'll be sworn, by what I see of you, you are not:—To the bottom;—I warrant him a true church-man.—Now, father, to our business: 'tis agreeable to your calling; I do intend to do an act of charity.

Father DOMINICK
And I love to hear of charity; 'tis a comfortable subject.

LORENZO
Being in the late battle, in great hazard of my life, I recommended my person to good Saint Dominick.

Father DOMINICK
You could not have pitched upon a better; he's a sure card; I never knew him fail his votaries.

LORENZO
Troth, I also made bold to strike up a bargain with him, that, if I escaped with life and plunder, I would present some brother of his order with part of the booty taken from the infidels, to be employed in charitable uses.

Father DOMINICK
There you hit him; Saint Dominick loves charity exceedingly; that argument never fails with him.

LORENZO
The spoils were mighty; and I scorn to wrong him of a farthing. To make short my story; I inquired among the jacobins for an almoner, and the general fame has pointed out your reverence as the worthiest man:—here are fifty good pieces in this purse.

Father DOMINICK
How, fifty pieces? 'tis too much, too much in conscience.

LORENZO
Here, take them, father.

Father DOMINICK
No, in troth, I dare not; do not tempt me to break my vow of poverty.

LORENZO
If you are modest, I must force you; for I am strongest.

Father DOMINICK
Nay, if you compel me, there's no contending; but, will you set your strength against a decrepit, poor, old man?

[Takes the Purse.]

As I said, 'tis too great a bounty; but Saint Dominick shall owe you another scape: I'll put him in mind of you.

LORENZO
If you please, father, we will not trouble him 'till the next battle. But you may do me a greater kindness, by conveying my prayers to a female saint.

Father DOMINICK
A female saint! good now, good now, how your devotions jump with mine! I always loved the female saints.

LORENZO
I mean, a female, mortal, married-woman-saint: Look upon the superscription of this note; you know Don Gomez's wife.

[Gives him a Letter.]

Father DOMINICK
Who? Donna Elvira? I think I have some reason; I am her ghostly father.

LORENZO
I have some business of importance with her, which I have communicated in this paper; but her husband is so horribly given to be jealous,—

Father DOMINICK
Ho, jealous? he's the very quintessence of jealousy; he keeps no male creature in his house; and from abroad he lets no man come near her.

LORENZO
Excepting you, father.

Father DOMINICK
Me, I grant you; I am her director and her guide in spiritual affairs: But he has his humours with me too; for t'other day he called me false apostle.

LORENZO
Did he so? that reflects upon you all; on my word, father, that touches your copy-hold. If you would do a meritorious action, you might revenge the church's quarrel.—My letter, father,—

Father DOMINICK
Well, so far as a letter, I will take upon me; for what can I refuse to a man so charitably given?

LORENZO
If you bring an answer back, that purse in your hand has a twin-brother, as like him as ever he can look; there are fifty pieces lie dormant in it, for more charities.

Father DOMINICK
That must not be; not a farthing more, upon my priesthood.—But what may be the purport and meaning of this letter? that, I confess, a little troubles me.

LORENZO
No harm, I warrant you.

Father DOMINICK
Well, you are a charitable man; and I'll take your word: my comfort is, I know not the contents; and so far I am blameless. But an answer you shall have; though not for the sake of your fifty pieces more: I have sworn not to take them; they shall not be altogether fifty. Your mistress—forgive me, that I should call her your mistress, I meant Elvira,—lives but at next door: I'll visit her immediately; but not a word more of the nine-and-forty pieces.

LORENZO
Nay, I'll wait on you down stairs.—Fifty pounds for the postage of a letter! to send by the church is certainly the dearest road in Christendom.

[Exeunt.

SCENE III.—A Chamber

Enter **GOMEZ** and **ELVIRA**.

GOMEZ
Henceforth I banish flesh and wine: I'll have none stirring within these walls these twelve months.

ELVIRA
I care not; the sooner I am starved, the sooner I am rid of wedlock. I shall learn the knack to fast o' days; you have used me to fasting nights already.

GOMEZ
How the gipsey answers me! Oh, 'tis a most notorious hilding.

ELVIRA [Crying.]
But was ever poor innocent creature so hardly dealt with, for a little harmless chat?

GOMEZ
Oh, the impudence of this wicked sex! Lascivious dialogues are innocent with you!

ELVIRA
Was it such a crime to inquire how the battle passed?

GOMEZ
But that was not the business, gentlewoman: you were not asking news of a battle passed; you were engaging for a skirmish that was to come.

ELVIRA
An honest woman would be glad to hear, that her honour was safe, and her enemies were slain.

GOMEZ [In her tone.]
And to ask, if he were wounded in your defence; and, in case he were, to offer yourself to be his chirurgeon;—then, you did not describe your husband to him, for a covetous, jealous, rich, old hunks.

ELVIRA
No, I need not; he describes himself sufficiently: but, in what dream did I do this?

GOMEZ
You walked in your sleep, with your eyes broad open, at noon-day; and dreamt you were talking to the foresaid purpose with one Colonel Hernando—

ELVIRA
Who, dear husband, who?

GOMEZ
What the devil have I said?—You would have farther information, would you?

ELVIRA
No; but my dear, little, old man, tell me now, that I may avoid him for your sake.

GOMEZ

Get you up into your chamber, cockatrice; and there immure yourself; be confined, I say, during our royal pleasure. But, first, down on your marrowbones, upon your allegiance, and make an acknowledgement of your offences; for I will have ample satisfaction.

[Pulls her down.

ELVIRA
I have done you no injury, and therefore I'll make you no submission: but I'll complain to my ghostly father.

GOMEZ
Ay, there's your remedy; when you receive condign punishment, you run with open mouth to your confessor; that parcel of holy guts and garbadge: he must chuckle you and moan you; but I'll rid my hands of his ghostly authority one day,

[Enter **Father DOMINICK**.]

—and make him know he's the son of a—[Sees him.] So;—no sooner conjure, but the devil's in the circle.

Father DOMINICK
Son of a what, Don Gomez?

GOMEZ
Why, a son of a church; I hope there's no harm in that, father?

Father DOMINICK
I will lay up your words for you, till time shall serve; and to-morrow I enjoin you to fast, for penance.

GOMEZ
There's no harm in that; she shall fast too: fasting saves money. [Aside.

Father DOMINICK[To **ELVIRA**.]
What was the reason that I found you upon your knees, in that unseemly posture?

GOMEZ
O horrible! to find a woman upon her knees, he says, is an unseemly posture; there's a priest for you! [Aside.

ELVIRA [To**Father DOMINICK**]
I wish, father, you would give me an opportunity of entertaining you in private: I have somewhat upon my spirits that presses me exceedingly.

Father DOMINICK
This goes well: [Aside.] Gomez, stand you at a distance,—farther yet,—stand out of ear shot;—I have somewhat to say to your wife in private.

GOMEZ
Was ever man thus priest-ridden? would the steeple of his church were in his belly: I am sure there's room for it. [Aside.

ELVIRA
I am ashamed to acknowledge my infirmities; but you have been always an indulgent father, and therefore I will venture to—and yet I dare not!—

Father DOMINICK
Nay, if you are bashful;—if you keep your wound from the knowledge of your surgeon,—

ELVIRA
You know my husband is a man in years; but he's my husband, and therefore I shall be silent; but his humours are more intolerable than his age: he's grown so froward, so covetous, and so jealous, that he has turned my heart quite from him; and, if I durst confess it, has forced me to cast my affections on another man.

Father DOMINICK
Good:—hold, hold; I meant abominable.—Pray heaven this may be my colonel!   [Aside.

ELVIRA
I have seen this man, father, and have encouraged his addresses; he's a young gentleman, a soldier, of a most winning carriage: and what his courtship may produce at last, I know not; but I am afraid of my own frailty.

Father DOMINICK
'Tis he, for certain;—she has saved the credit of my function, by speaking first; now must I take gravity upon me. [Aside.

GOMEZ
This whispering bodes me no good, for certain; but he has me so plaguily under the lash, that I dare not interrupt him. [Aside.

Father DOMINICK
Daughter, daughter, do you remember your matrimonial vow?

ELVIRA
Yes, to my sorrow, father, I do remember it; a miserable woman it has made me: but you know, father, a marriage-vow is but a thing of course, which all women take when they would get a husband.

Father DOMINICK
A vow is a very solemn thing; and 'tis good to keep it: but, notwithstanding, it may be broken upon some occasions. Have you striven with all your might against this frailty?

ELVIRA
Yes, I have striven; but I found it was against the stream. Love, you know, father, is a great vow-maker; but he's a greater vow-breaker.

Father DOMINICK
'Tis your duty to strive always; but, notwithstanding, when we have done our utmost, it extenuates the sin.

GOMEZ
I can hold no longer.—Now, gentlewoman, you are confessing your enormities; I know it, by that hypocritical downcast look:—enjoin her to sit bare upon a bed of nettles, father; you can do no less, in conscience.

Father DOMINICK
Hold your peace; are you growing malapert? will you force me to make use of my authority? your wife's a well disposed and a virtuous lady; I say it, In verbo sacerdotis.

ELVIRA
I know not what to do, father; I find myself in a most desperate condition; and so is the colonel, for love of me.

Father DOMINICK
The colonel, say you! I wish it be not the same young gentleman I know. 'Tis a gallant young man, I must confess, worthy of any lady's love in Christendom,—in a lawful way, I mean: of such a charming behaviour, so bewitching to a woman's eye, and, furthermore, so charitably given; by all good tokens, this must be my colonel Hernando.

ELVIRA
Ay, and my colonel too, father:—I am overjoyed!—and are you then acquainted with him?

Father DOMINICK
Acquainted with him! why, he haunts me up and down; and, I am afraid, it is for love of you; for he pressed a letter upon me, within this hour, to deliver to you. I confess I received it, lest he should send it by some other; but with full resolution never to put it into your hands.

ELVIRA
Oh, dear father, let me have it, or I shall die!

GOMEZ
Whispering still! A pox of your close committee! I'll listen, I'm resolved.

[Steals nearer.

Father DOMINICK
Nay, if you are obstinately bent to see it, use your discretion; but, for my part, I wash my hands of it.—What makes you listening there? get farther off; I preach not to thee, thou wicked eaves dropper.

ELVIRA
I'll kneel down, father, as if I were taking absolution, if you'll but please to stand before me.

Father DOMINICK

At your peril be it then. I have told you the ill consequences; et liberavi animam meam. Your reputation is in danger, to say nothing of your soul. Notwithstanding, when the spiritual means have been applied, and fail, in that case the carnal may be used. You are a tender child, you are, and must not be put into despair; your heart is as soft and melting as your hand.

[He strokes her face, takes her by the hand, and gives the letter.

GOMEZ
Hold, hold, father, you go beyond your commission; palming is always held foul play amongst gamesters.

Father DOMINICK
Thus good intentions are misconstrued by wicked men; you will never be warned till you are excommunicated.

GOMEZ
Ah, devil on him; there's his hold! If there were no more in excommunication than the church's censure, a wise man would lick his conscience whole with a wet finger; but, if I am excommunicated, I am outlawed, and then there is no calling in my money. [Aside.

ELVIRA [Rising.]
I have read the note, father, and will send him an answer immediately; for I know his lodgings by his letter.

Father DOMINICK
I understand it not, for my part; but I wish your intentions be honest. Remember, that adultery, though it be a silent sin, yet it is a crying sin also. Nevertheless, if you believe absolutely he will die, unless you pity him; to save a man's life is a point of charity; and actions of charity do alleviate, as I may say, and take off from the mortality of the sin. Farewell, daughter.—Gomez, cherish your virtuous wife; and thereupon I give you my benediction.

[Going.

GOMEZ
Stay; I'll conduct you to the door,—that I may be sure you steal nothing by the way. Friars wear not their long sleeves for nothing.—Oh, 'tis a Judas Iscariot.

[Exit after the **FRIAR**.

ELVIRA
This friar is a comfortable man! He will understand nothing of the business, and yet does it all.
Pray, wives and virgins, at your time of need, For a true guide, of my good father's breed.

[Exit.

ACT III

SCENE I.—The Street

Enter **LORENZO** in a Friars Habit, meeting **Father DOMINICK**.

LORENZO
Father Dominick, father Dominick; why in such haste, man?

Father DOMINICK
It should seem, a brother of our order.

LORENZO
No, faith, I am only your brother in iniquity; my holiness, like yours, is mere outside.

Father DOMINICK
What! my noble colonel in metamorphosis! On what occasion are you transformed?

LORENZO
Love, almighty love; that, which turned Jupiter into a town-bull, has transformed me into a friar. I have had a letter from Elvira, in answer to that I sent by you.

Father DOMINICK
You see I have delivered my message faithfully; I am a friar of honour, where I am engaged.

LORENZO
O, I understand your hint; the other fifty pieces are ready to be condemned to charity.

Father DOMINICK
But this habit, son! this habit!

LORENZO
It is a habit, that, in all ages, has been friendly to fornication: you have begun the design in this clothing, and I'll try to accomplish it. The husband is absent, that evil counsellor is removed and the sovereign is graciously disposed to hear my grievances.

Father DOMINICK
Go to, go to; I find good counsel is but thrown away upon you.
Fare you well, fare you well, son! Ah—

LORENZO
How! will you turn recreant at the last cast? You must along to countenance my undertaking: we are at the door, man.

Father DOMINICK
Well, I have thought on't, and I will not go.

LORENZO

You may stay, father, but no fifty pounds without it; that was only promised in the bond: "But the condition of this obligation is such, that if the above-named father, father Dominick, do not well and faithfully perform—"

Father DOMINICK
Now I better think on't, I will bear you company; for the reverence of my presence may be a curb to your exorbitancies.

LORENZO
Lead up your myrmidons, and enter.

[Exeunt.

SCENE II.—Elvira's Chamber

Enter **ELVIRA**.

ELVIRA
He'll come, that's certain; young appetites are sharp, and seldom need twice bidding to such a banquet. Well, if I prove frail,—as I hope I shall not till I have compassed my design,—never woman had such a husband to provoke her, such a lover to allure her, or such a confessor to absolve her. Of what am I afraid, then? not my conscience, that's safe enough; my ghostly father has given it a dose of church-opium, to lull it. Well, for soothing sin, I'll say that for him, he's a chaplain for any court in Christendom.

[Enter **LORENZO** and **Father DOMINICK**.

O, father Dominick, what news?—How, a companion with you! What game have you in hand, that you hunt in couples?

LORENZO [Lifting up his Hood.]
I'll shew you that immediately.

ELVIRA
O, my love!

LORENZO
My life!

ELVIRA
My soul!

[They embrace.

Father DOMINICK
I am taken on the sudden with a grievous swimming in my head, and such a mist before my eyes, that I can neither hear nor see.

ELVIRA
Stay, and I'll fetch you some comfortable water.

Father DOMINICK
No, no; nothing but the open air will do me good. I'll take a turn in your garden; but remember that I trust you both, and do not wrong my good opinion of you.

[Exit **Father DOMINICK**.

ELVIRA
This is certainly the dust of gold which you have thrown in the good man's eyes, that on the sudden he cannot see; for my mind misgives me, this sickness of his is but apocryphal.

LORENZO
'Tis no qualm of conscience, I'll be sworn. You see, madam, it is interest governs all the world. He preaches against sin; why? because he gets by it: He holds his tongue; why? because so much more is bidden for his silence.

ELVIRA
And so much for the friar.

LORENZO
Oh, those eyes of yours reproach me justly, that I neglect the subject which brought me hither.

ELVIRA
Do you consider the hazard I have run to see you here? if you do, methinks it should inform you, that I love not at a common rate.

LORENZO
Nay, if you talk of considering, let us consider why we are alone. Do you think the friar left us together to tell beads? Love is a kind of penurious god, very niggardly of his opportunities: he must be watched like a hard-hearted treasurer; for he bolts out on the sudden, and, if you take him not in the nick, he vanishes in a twinkling.

ELVIRA
Why do you make such haste to have done loving me? You men are all like watches, wound up for striking twelve immediately; but after you are satisfied, the very next that follows, is the solitary sound of a single—one!

LORENZO
How, madam! do you invite me to a feast, and then preach abstinence?

ELVIRA
No, I invite you to a feast where the dishes are served up in order: you are for making a hasty meal, and for chopping up your entertainment, like a hungry clown. Trust my management, good colonel, and call not for your desert too soon: believe me, that which comes last, as it is the sweetest, so it cloys the soonest.

LORENZO
I perceive, madam, by your holding me at this distance, that there is somewhat you expect from me: what am I to undertake, or suffer, ere I can be happy?

ELVIRA
I must first be satisfied, that you love me.

LORENZO
By all that's holy! by these dear eyes!—

ELVIRA
Spare your oaths and protestations; I know you gallants of the time have a mint at your tongue's end to coin them.

LORENZO
You know you cannot marry me; but, by heavens, if you were in a condition—

ELVIRA
Then you would not be so prodigal of your promises, but have the fear of matrimony before your eyes. In few words, if you love me, as you profess, deliver me from this bondage, take me out of Egypt, and I'll wander with you as far as earth, and seas, and love, can carry us.

LORENZO
I never was out at a mad frolic, though this is the maddest I ever undertook. Have with you, lady mine; I take you at your word; and if you are for a merry jaunt, I'll try for once who can foot it farthest. There are hedges in summer, and barns in winter, to be found; I with my knapsack, and you with your bottle at your back: we will leave honour to madmen, and riches to knaves; and travel till we come to' the ridge of the world, and then drop together into the next.

ELVIRA
Give me your hand, and strike a bargain.

[He takes her hand, and kisses it.

LORENZO
In sign and token whereof, the parties interchangeably, and so forth.—When should I be weary of sealing upon this soft wax?

ELVIRA
O heavens! I hear my husband's voice.

[Enter **GOMEZ.**

GOMEZ
Where are you, gentlewoman? there's something in the wind, I'm sure, because your woman would have run up stairs before me; but I have secured her below, with a gag in her chaps.—Now, in the devil's

name, what makes this friar here again? I do not like these frequent conjunctions of the flesh and spirit; they are boding.

ELVIRA
Go hence, good father; my husband, you see, is in an ill humour, and I would not have you witness of his folly.

[LORENZO going.

GOMEZ [Running to the door.]
By your reverence's favour, hold a little; I must examine you something better, before you go.—Heyday! who have we here? Father Dominick is shrunk in the wetting two yards and a half about the belly. What are become of those two timber logs, that he used to wear for legs, that stood strutting like the two black posts before a door? I am afraid some bad body has been setting him over a fire in a great cauldron, and boiled him down half the quantity, for a recipe. This is no father Dominick, no huge overgrown abbey-lubber; this is but a diminutive sucking friar. As sure as a gun, now, father Dominick has been spawning this young slender anti-christ.

ELVIRA
He will be found, there's no prevention. [Aside.

GOMEZ
Why does he not speak? What! is the friar possessed with a dumb devil? if he be, I shall make bold to conjure him.

ELVIRA
He is but a novice in his order, and is enjoined silence for a penance.

GOMEZ
A novice, quotha! you would make a novice of me, too, if you could. But what was his business here? answer me that, gentlewoman, answer me that.

ELVIRA
What should it be, but to give me some spiritual instructions.

GOMEZ
Very good; and you are like to edify much from a dumb preacher. This will not pass, I must examine the contents of him a little closer.—O thou confessor, confess who thou art, or thou art no friar of this world!—

[He comes to **LORENZO**, who struggles with him; his Habit flies open, and discovers a Sword; **GOMEZ** starts back.]

—As I live, this is a manifest member of the church militant.

LORENZO [Aside.]
I am discovered; now, impudence be my refuge.—Yes, faith, 'tis I, honest Gomez; thou seest I use thee like a friend; this is a familiar visit.

GOMEZ
What! colonel Hernando turned a friar! who could have suspected you of so much godliness?

LORENZO
Even as thou seest, I make bold here.

GOMEZ
A very frank manner of proceeding; but I do not wonder at your visit, after so friendly an invitation as I made you. Marry, I hope you will excuse the blunderbusses for not being in readiness to salute you; but let me know your hour, and all shall be mended another time.

LORENZO
Hang it, I hate such ripping up of old unkindness: I was upon the frolic this evening, and came to visit thee in masquerade.

GOMEZ
Very likely; and not finding me at home, you were forced to toy away an hour with my wife, or so.

LORENZO
Right; thou speak'st my very soul.

GOMEZ
Why, am not I a friend, then, to help thee out? you would have been fumbling half an hour for this excuse. But, as I remember, you promised to storm my citadel, and bring your regiment of red locusts upon me for free quarters: I find, colonel, by your habit, there are black locusts in the world, as well as red.

ELVIRA [Aside.
When comes my share of the reckoning to be called for?

LORENZO
Give me thy hand; thou art the honestest, kind man!—I was resolved I would not out of thy house till I had seen thee.

GOMEZ
No, in my conscience, if I had staid abroad till midnight. But, colonel, you and I shall talk in another tone hereafter; I mean, in cold friendship, at a bar before a judge, by the way of plaintiff and defendant. Your excuses want some grains to make them current: Hum, and ha, will not do the business.—There's a modest lady of your acquaintance, she has so much grace to make none at all, but silently to confess the power of dame Nature working in her body to youthful appetite.

ELVIRA
How he got in I know not, unless it were by virtue of his habit.

GOMEZ
Ay, ay, the virtues of that habit are known abundantly.

ELVIRA
I could not hinder his entrance, for he took me unprovided.

GOMEZ
To resist him.

ELVIRA
I'm sure he has not been here above a quarter of an hour.

GOMEZ
And a quarter of that time would have served the turn. O thou epitome of thy virtuous sex! Madam Messalina the second, retire to thy apartment: I have an assignation there to make with thee.

ELVIRA
I am all obedience.

[Exit **ELVIRA**.

LORENZO
I find, Gomez, you are not the man I thought you. We may meet before we come to the bar, we may; and our differences may be decided by other weapons than by lawyers' tongues. In the mean time, no ill treatment of your wife, as you hope to die a natural death, and go to hell in your bed. Bilbo is the word, remember that and tremble.—

[He's going out.

[Enter **Father DOMINICK**.

Father DOMINICK
Where is this naughty couple? where are you, in the name of goodness? My mind misgave me, and I durst trust you no longer with yourselves: Here will be fine work, I'm afraid, at your next confession.

LORENZO [Aside.]
The devil is punctual, I see; he has paid me the shame he owed me; and now the friar is coming in for his part too.

Father DOMINICK [Seeing **GOMEZ**.]
Bless my eyes! what do I see?

GOMEZ
Why, you see a cuckold of this honest gentleman's making; I thank him for his pains.

Father DOMINICK
I confess, I am astonished!

GOMEZ
What, at a cuckoldom of your own contrivance! your head-piece, and his limbs, have done my business. Nay, do not look so strangely; remember your own words,—Here will be fine work at your next

confession. What naughty couple were they whom you durst not trust together any longer?—when the hypocritical rogue had trusted them a full quarter of an hour;—and, by the way, horns will sprout in less time than mushrooms.

Father DOMINICK
Beware how you accuse one of my order upon light suspicions. The naughty couple, that I meant, were your wife and you, whom I left together with great animosities on both sides. Now, that was the occasion,—mark me, Gomez,—that I thought it convenient to return again, and not to trust your enraged spirits too long together. You might have broken out into revilings and matrimonial warfare, which are sins; and new sins make work for new confessions.

LORENZO [Aside.
Well said, i'faith, friar; thou art come off thyself, but poor I am left in limbo.

GOMEZ
Angle in some other ford, good father, you shall catch no gudgeons here. Look upon the prisoner at the bar, friar, and inform the court what you know concerning him; he is arraigned here by the name of colonel Hernando.

Father DOMINICK
What colonel do you mean, Gomez? I see no man but a reverend brother of our order, whose profession I honour, but whose person I know not, as I hope for paradise.

GOMEZ
No, you are not acquainted with him, the more's the pity; you do not know him, under this disguise, for the greatest cuckold-maker in all Spain.

Father DOMINICK
O impudence! O rogue! O villain! Nay, if he be such a man, my
righteous spirit rises at him! Does he put on holy garments, for a
cover-shame of lewdness?

GOMEZ
Yes, and he's in the right on't, father: when a swinging sin is to be committed, nothing will cover it so close as a friar's hood; for there the devil plays at bo-peep,—puts out his horns to do a mischief, and then shrinks them back for safety, like a snail into her shell.

LORENZO
It's best marching off, while I can retreat with honour. There's no trusting this friar's conscience; he has renounced me already more heartily than e'er he did the devil, and is in a fair way to prosecute me for putting on these holy robes. This is the old church-trick; the clergy is ever at the bottom of the plot, but they are wise enough to slip their own necks out of the collar, and leave the laity to be fairly hanged for it.

[Aside and exit.

GOMEZ

Follow your leader, friar; your colonel is trooped off, but he had not gone so easily, if I durst have trusted you in the house behind me. Gather up your gouty legs, I say, and rid my house of that huge body of divinity.

Father DOMINICK
I expect some judgment should fall upon you, for your want of reverence to your spiritual director: Slander, covetousness, and jealousy, will weigh thee down.

GOMEZ
Put pride, hypocrisy, and gluttony into your scale, father, and you shall weigh against me: Nay, an sins come to be divided once, the clergy puts in for nine parts, and scarce leaves the laity a tithe.

Father DOMINICK
How dar'st thou reproach the tribe of Levi?

GOMEZ
Marry, because you make us laymen of the tribe of Issachar. You make asses of us, to bear your burthens. When we are young, you put panniers upon us with your church-discipline; and when we are grown up, you load us with a wife: after that, you procure for other men, and then you load our wives too. A fine phrase you have amongst you to draw us into marriage, you call it—settling of a man; just as when a fellow has got a sound knock upon the head, they say—he's settled: Marriage is a settling-blow indeed. They say every thing in the world is good for something; as a toad, to suck up the venom of the earth; but I never knew what a friar was good for, till your pimping shewed me.

Father DOMINICK
Thou shalt answer for this, thou slanderer; thy offences be upon thy head.

GOMEZ
I believe there are some offences there of your planting.

[Exit **Father DOMINICK**.]

Lord, Lord, that men should have sense enough to set snares in their warrens to catch polecats and foxes, and yet—Want wit a priest-trap at their door to lay, For holy vermin that in houses prey.

[Exit **GOMEZ**.

SCENE III.—A Bed Chamber

LEONORA, and **TERESA**.

TERESA
You are not what you were, since yesterday;
Your food forsakes you, and your needful rest;
You pine, you languish, love to be alone;
Think much, speak little, and, in speaking, sigh:

When you see Torrismond, you are unquiet;
But, when you see him not, you are in pain.

LEONORA
O let them never love, who never tried!
They brought a paper to me to be signed;
Thinking on him, I quite forgot my name,
And writ, for Leonora, Torrismond.
I went to bed, and to myself I thought
That I would think on Torrismond no more;
Then shut my eyes, but could not shut out him.
I turned, and tried each corner of my bed,
To find if sleep were there, but sleep was lost.
Fev'rish, for want of rest, I rose, and walked,
And, by the moon-shine, to the windows went;
There, thinking to exclude him from my thoughts,
I cast my eyes upon the neighbouring fields,
And, ere I was aware, sighed to myself,—
There fought my Torrismond.

TERESA
What hinders you to take the man you love?
The people will be glad, the soldiers shout,
And Bertran, though repining, will be awed.

LEONORA
I fear to try new love,
As boys to venture on the unknown ice,
That crackles underneath them while they slide.
Oh, how shall I describe this growing ill!
Betwixt my doubt and love, methinks I stand
Altering, like one that waits an ague fit;
And yet, would this were all!

TERESA
What fear you more?

LEONORA
I am ashamed to say, 'tis but a fancy.
At break of day, when dreams, they say, are true,
A drowzy slumber, rather than a sleep,
Seized on my senses, with long watching worn:
Methought I stood on a wide river's bank,
Which I must needs o'erpass, but knew not how;
When, on a sudden, Torrismond appeared,
Gave me his hand, and led me lightly o'er,
Leaping and bounding on the billows' heads,
'Till safely we had reached the farther shore.

TERESA
This dream portends some ill which you shall 'scape.
Would you see fairer visions, take this night
Your Torrismond within your arms to sleep;
And, to that end, invent some apt pretence
To break with Bertran: 'twould be better yet,
Could you provoke him to give you the occasion,
And then, to throw him off.

[Enter **BERTRAN** at a distance.

LEONORA
My stars have sent him;
For, see, he comes. How gloomily he looks!
If he, as I suspect, have found my love,
His jealousy will furnish him with fury,
And me with means, to part.

BERTRAN [Aside.]
Shall I upbraid her? Shall I call her false?
If she be false, 'tis what she most desires.
My genius whispers me,—Be cautious, Bertran!
Thou walkest as on a narrow mountain's neck,
A dreadful height, with scanty room to tread.

LEONORA
What business have you at the court, my lord?

BERTRAN
What business, madam?

LEONORA
Yes, my lord, what business?
'Tis somewhat, sure, of weighty consequence,
That brings you here so often, and unsent for.

BERTRAN
'Tis what I feared; her words are cold enough,
To freeze a man to death. [Aside.]—May I presume
To speak, and to complain?

LEONORA
They, who complain to princes, think them tame:
What bull dares bellow, or what sheep dares bleat,
Within the lion's den?

BERTRAN

Yet men are suffered to put heaven in mind
Of promised blessings; for they then are debts.

LEONORA
My lord, heaven knows its own time when to give;
But you, it seems, charge me with breach of faith!

BERTRAN
I hope I need not, madam;
But as, when men in sickness lingering lie,
They count the tedious hours by months and years,—
So, every day deferred, to dying lovers,
Is a whole age of pain!

LEONORA
What if I ne'er consent to make you mine?
My father's promise ties me not to time;
And bonds, without a date, they say, are void.

BERTRAN
Far be it from me to believe you bound;
Love is the freest motion of our minds:
O could you see into my secret soul,
There might you read your own dominion doubled,
Both as a queen and mistress. If you leave me,
Know I can die, but dare not be displeased.

LEONORA
Sure you affect stupidity, my lord;
Or give me cause to think, that, when you lost
Three battles to the Moors, you coldly stood
As unconcerned as now.

BERTRAN
I did my best;
Fate was not in my power.

LEONORA
And, with the like tame gravity, you saw
A raw young warrior take your baffled work,
And end it at a blow.

BERTRAN
I humbly take my leave; but they, who blast
Your good opinion of me, may have cause
To know, I am no coward.

[He is going.

LEONORA
Bertran, stay.
[Aside.] This may produce some dismal consequence
To him, whom dearer than my life I love.
[To him.] Have I not managed my contrivance well,
To try your love, and make you doubt of mine?

BERTRAN
Then, was it but a trial?
Methinks I start as from some dreadful dream,
And often ask myself if yet I wake.—
This turn's too quick to be without design;
I'll sound the bottom of't, ere I believe. [Aside.

LEONORA
I find your love, and would reward it too,
But anxious fears solicit my weak breast.
I fear my people's faith;
That hot-mouthed beast, that bears against the curb,
Hard to be broken even by lawful kings,
But harder by usurpers.
Judge then, my lord, with all these cares opprest,
If I can think of love.

BERTRAN
Believe me, madam,
These jealousies, however large they spread,
Have but one root, the old imprisoned king;
Whose lenity first pleased the gaping crowd;
But when long tried, and found supinely good,
Like Æsop's Log, they leapt upon his back.
Your father knew them well; and, when he mounted,
He reined them strongly, and he spurred them hard:
And, but he durst not do it all at once,
He had not left alive this patient saint,
This anvil of affronts, but sent him hence
To hold a peaceful branch of palm above,
And hymn it in the quire.

LEONORA
You've hit upon the very string, which, touched.
Echoes the sound, and jars within my soul;—
There lies my grief.

BERTRAN
So long as there's a head,
Thither will all the mounting spirits fly;

Lop that but off, and then—

LEONORA
My virtue shrinks from such an horrid act.

BERTRAN
This 'tis to have a virtue out of season.
Mercy is good, a very good dull virtue;
But kings mistake its timing, and are mild,
When manly courage bids them be severe:
Better be cruel once, than anxious ever.
Remove this threatening danger from your crown,
And then securely take the man you love.

LEONORA [Walking aside.]
Ha! let me think of that:—The man I love?
'Tis true, this murder is the only means,
That can secure my throne to Torrismond:
Nay, more, this execution, done by Bertran,
Makes him the object of the people's hate.

BERTRAN [Aside.]
The more she thinks, 'twill work the stronger in her.

LEONORA
How eloquent is mischief to persuade!
Few are so wicked, as to take delight
In crimes unprofitable, nor do I:
If then I break divine and human laws,
No bribe but love could gain so bad a cause. [Aside.

BERTRAN
You answer nothing.

LEONORA
'Tis of deep concernment,
And I a woman, ignorant and weak:
I leave it all to you; think, what you do,
You do for him I love.

BERTRAN
For him she loves?
She named not me; that may be Torrismond,
Whom she has thrice in private seen this day;
Then I am fairly caught in my own snare.
I'll think again. [Aside.]—Madam, it shall be done;
And mine be all the blame.

[Exit.

LEONORA
O, that it were! I would not do this crime,
And yet, like heaven, permit it to be done.
The priesthood grossly cheat us with free-will:
Will to do what—but what heaven first decreed?
Our actions then are neither good nor ill,
Since from eternal causes they proceed;
Our passions,—fear and anger, love and hate,—
Mere senseless engines that are moved by fate;
Like ships on stormy seas, without a guide,
Tost by the winds, and driven by the tide.

[Enter **TORRISMOND**.

TORRISMOND
Am I not rudely bold, and press too often
Into your presence, madam? If I am—

LEONORA
No more, lest I should chide you for your stay:
Where have you been? and how could you suppose,
That I could live these two long hours without you?

TORRISMOND
O words, to charm an angel from his orb!
Welcome, as kindly showers to long-parched earth!
But I have been in such a dismal place,
Where joy ne'er enters, which the sun ne'er cheers,
Bound in with darkness, overspread with damps;
Where I have seen (if I could say I saw)
The good old king, majestic in his bonds,
And, 'midst his griefs, most venerably great:
By a dim winking lamp, which feebly broke
The gloomy vapours, he lay stretched along
Upon the unwholesome earth, his eyes fixed upward;
And ever and anon a silent tear
Stole down, and trickled from his hoary beard.

LEONORA
O heaven, what have I done!—my gentle love,
Here end thy sad discourse, and, for my sake,
Cast off these fearful melancholy thoughts.

TORRISMOND
My heart is withered at that piteous sight,
As early blossoms are with eastern blasts:

He sent for me, and, while I raised his head,
He threw his aged arms about my neck;
And, seeing that I wept, he pressed me close:
So, leaning cheek to cheek, and eyes to eyes,
We mingled tears in a dumb scene of sorrow.

LEONORA
Forbear; you know not how you wound my soul.

TORRISMOND
Can you have grief, and not have pity too?
He told me,—when my father did return,
He had a wond'rous secret to disclose:
He kissed me, blessed me, nay—he called me son;
He praised my courage; prayed for my success:
He was so true a father of his country,
To thank me, for defending even his foes,
Because they were his subjects.

LEONORA
If they be,—then what am I?

TORRISMOND
The sovereign of my soul, my earthly heaven.

LEONORA
And not your queen?

TORRISMOND
You are so beautiful,
So wond'rous fair, you justify rebellion;
As if that faultless face could make no sin,
But heaven, with looking on it, must forgive.

LEONORA
The king must die,—he must, my Torrismond,
Though pity softly plead within my soul;
Yet he must die, that I may make you great,
And give a crown in dowry with my love.

TORRISMOND
Perish that crown—on any head but yours!
O, recollect your thoughts!
Shake not his hour-glass, when his hasty sand
Is ebbing to the last:
A little longer, yet a little longer,
And nature drops him down, without your sin;
Like mellow fruit, without a winter storm.

LEONORA
Let me but do this one injustice more.
His doom is past, and, for your sake, he dies.

TORRISMOND
Would you, for me, have done so ill an act,
And will not do a good one!
Now, by your joys on earth, your hopes in heaven,
O spare this great, this good, this aged king;
And spare your soul the crime!

LEONORA
The crime's not mine;
'Twas first proposed, and must be done, by Bertran,
Fed with false hopes to gain my crown and me;
I, to enhance his ruin, gave no leave,
But barely bade him think, and then resolve.

TORRISMOND
In not forbidding, you command the crime:
Think, timely think, on the last dreadful day;
How will you tremble, there to stand exposed,
And foremost, in the rank of guilty ghosts,
That must be doomed for murder! think on murder:
That troop is placed apart from common crimes;
The damned themselves start wide, and shun that band,
As far more black, and more forlorn than they.

LEONORA
'Tis terrible! it shakes, it staggers me;
I knew this truth, but I repelled that thought.
Sure there is none, but fears a future state;
And, when the most obdurate swear they do not,
Their trembling hearts belie their boasting tongues.

[Enter **TERESA**.

Send speedily to Bertran; charge him strictly
Not to proceed, but wait my farther pleasure.

TERESA
Madam, he sends to tell you, 'tis performed.

[Exit.

TORRISMOND
Ten thousand plagues consume him! furies drag him,

Fiends tear him! blasted be the arm that struck,
The tongue that ordered!—only she be spared,
That hindered not the deed! O, where was then
The power, that guards the sacred lives of kings?
Why slept the lightning and the thunder-bolts,
Or bent their idle rage on fields and trees,
When vengeance called them here?

LEONORA
Sleep that thought too;
'Tis done, and, since 'tis done, 'tis past recal;
And, since 'tis past recal, must be forgotten.

TORRISMOND
O, never, never, shall it be forgotten!
High heaven will not forget it; after-ages
Shall with a fearful curse remember ours;
And blood shall never leave the nation more!

LEONORA
His body shall be royally interred,
And the last funeral-pomps adorn his hearse;
I will myself (as I have cause too just,)
Be the chief mourner at his obsequies;
And yearly fix on the revolving day
The solemn marks of mourning, to atone,
And expiate my offence.

TORRISMOND
Nothing can,
But bloody vengeance on that traitor's head,—
Which, dear departed spirit, here I vow.

LEONORA
Here end our sorrows, and begin our joys:
Love calls, my Torrismond; though hate has raged,
And ruled the day, yet love will rule the night.
The spiteful stars have shed their venom down,
And now the peaceful planets take their turn.
This deed of Bertran's has removed all fears,
And given me just occasion to refuse him.
What hinders now, but that the holy priest
In secret join our mutual vows? and then
This night, this happy night, is yours and mine.

TORRISMOND
Be still my sorrows, and be loud my joys.
Fly to the utmost circles of the sea,

Thou furious tempest, that hast tossed my mind,
And leave no thought, but Leonora there.—
What's this I feel, a boding in my soul,
As if this day were fatal? be it so;
Fate shall but have the leavings of my love:
My joys are gloomy, but withal are great.
The lion, though he sees the toils are set,
Yet, pinched with raging hunger, scowers away,
Hunts in the face of danger all the day;
At night, with sullen pleasure, grumbles o'er his prey.

[Exeunt.

ACT IV

SCENE I.—Before Gomez's Door

Enter **LORENZO, Father DOMINICK,** and two **SOLDIERS** at a distance.

Father DOMINICK
I'll not wag an ace farther: the whole world shall not bribe me to it; for my conscience will digest these gross enormities no longer.

LORENZO
How, thy conscience not digest them! There is ne'er a friar in Spain can shew a conscience, that comes near it for digestion. It digested pimping, when I sent thee with my letter; and it digested perjury, when thou swor'st thou didst not know me: I am sure it has digested me fifty pounds, of as hard gold as is in all Barbary. Pr'ythee, why shouldest thou discourage fornication, when thou knowest thou lovest a sweet young girl?

Father DOMINICK
Away, away; I do not love them;—pah; no,—[spits.] I do not love a pretty girl—you are so waggish!—

[Spits again.

LORENZO
Why thy mouth waters at the very mention of them.

Father DOMINICK
You take a mighty pleasure in defamation, colonel; but I wonder what you find in running restless up and down, breaking your brains, emptying your purse, and wearing out your body, with hunting after unlawful game.

LORENZO
Why there's the satisfaction on't.

Father DOMINICK

This incontinency may proceed to adultery, and adultery to murder, and murder to hanging; and there's the satisfaction on't.

LORENZO

I'll not hang alone, friar; I'm resolved to peach thee before thy superiors, for what thou hast done already.

Father DOMINICK

I'm resolved to forswear it, if you do. Let me advise you better, colonel, than to accuse a church-man to a church-man; in the common cause we are all of a piece; we hang together.

LORENZO

If you don't, it were no matter if you did. [Aside.

Father DOMINICK

Nay, if you talk of peaching, I'll peach first, and see whose oath will be believed; I'll trounce you for offering to corrupt my honesty, and bribe my conscience: you shall be summoned by an host of parators; you shall be sentenced in the spiritual court; you shall be excommunicated; you shall be outlawed;—and—

[Here **LORENZO** takes a purse, and plays with it, and at last lets the purse fall chinking on the ground, which the **FRIAR** eyes.

[In another tone.] I say, a man might do this now, if he were maliciously disposed, and had a mind to bring matters to extremity: but, considering that you are my friend, a person of honour, and a worthy good charitable man, I would rather die a thousand deaths than disoblige you.

[**LORENZO** takes up the purse, and pours it into the Friar's sleeve.

Nay, good sir;—nay, dear colonel;—O lord, sir, what are you doing now! I profess this must not be: without this I would have served you to the utter-most; pray command me.—A jealous, foul-mouthed rogue this Gomez is; I saw how he used you, and you marked how he used me too. O he's a bitter man; but we'll join our forces; ah, shall we, colonel? we'll be revenged on him with a witness.

LORENZO

But how shall I send her word to be ready at the door? for I must reveal it in confession to you, that I mean to carry her away this evening, by the help of these two soldiers. I know Gomez suspects you, and you will hardly gain admittance.

Father DOMINICK

Let me alone; I fear him not. I am armed with the authority of my clothing: yonder I see him keeping sentry at his door:—have you never seen a citizen, in a cold morning, clapping his sides, and walking forward and backward, a mighty pace before his shop? but I'll gain the pass, in spite of his suspicion; stand you aside, and do but mark how I accost him.

LORENZO

If he meet with a repulse, we must throw off the fox's skin, and put on the lion's.—Come, gentlemen, you'll stand by me?

SOLDIER
Do not doubt us, colonel.

[They retire all three to a corner of the stage; **Father DOMINICK** goes to the door where **GOMEZ** stands.

Father DOMINICK
Good even, Gomez; how does your wife?

GOMEZ
Just as you'd have her; thinking on nothing but her dear colonel, and conspiring cuckoldom against me.

Father DOMINICK
I dare say, you wrong her; she is employing her thoughts how to cure you of your jealousy.

GOMEZ
Yes, by certainty.

Father DOMINICK
By your leave, Gomez; I have some spiritual advice to impart to her on that subject.

GOMEZ
You may spare your instructions, if you please, father; she has no farther need of them.

Father DOMINICK
How, no need of them! do you speak in riddles?

GOMEZ
Since you will have me speak plainer,—she has profited so well already by your counsel, that she can say her lesson without your teaching: Do you understand me now?

Father DOMINICK
I must not neglect my duty, for all that; once again, Gomez, by your leave.

GOMEZ
She's a little indisposed at present, and it will not be convenient to disturb her.

[**Father DOMINICK** offers to go by him, but t'other stands before him.

Father DOMINICK
Indisposed, say you? O, it is upon those occasions that a confessor is most necessary; I think, it was my good angel that sent me hither so opportunely.

GOMEZ
Ay, whose good angels sent you hither, that you best know, father.

Father DOMINICK
A word or two of devotion will do her no harm, I'm sure.

GOMEZ
A little sleep will do her more good, I'm sure: You know, she disburthened her conscience but this morning to you.

Father DOMINICK
But, if she be ill this afternoon, she may have new occasion to confess.

GOMEZ
Indeed, as you order matters with the colonel, she may have occasion of confessing herself every hour.

Father DOMINICK
Pray, how long has she been sick?

GOMEZ
Lord, you will force a man to speak;—why, ever since your last defeat.

Father DOMINICK
This can be but some slight indisposition; it will not last, and I may see her.

GOMEZ
How, not last! I say, it will last, and it shall last; she shall be sick these seven or eight days, and perhaps longer, as I see occasion. What? I know the mind of her sickness a little better than you do.

Father DOMINICK
I find, then, I must bring a doctor.

GOMEZ
And he'll bring an apothecary, with a chargeable long bill of ana's: those of my family have the grace to die cheaper. In a word, Sir Dominick, we understand one another's business here: I am resolved to stand like the Swiss of my own family, to defend the entrance; you may mumble over your pater nosters, if you please, and try if you can make my doors fly open, and batter down my walls with bell, book, and candle; but I am not of opinion, that you are holy enough to commit miracles.

Father DOMINICK
Men of my order are not to be treated after this manner.

GOMEZ
I would treat the pope and all his cardinals in the same manner, if they offered to see my wife, without my leave.

Father DOMINICK
I excommunicate thee from the church, if thou dost not open; there's promulgation coming out.

GOMEZ

And I excommunicate you from my wife, if you go to that: there's promulgation for promulgation, and bull for bull; and so I leave you to recreate yourself with the end of an old song—And sorrow came to the old friar.

[Exit.

[**LORENZO** comes to him.

LORENZO
I will not ask you your success; for I overheard part of it, and saw the conclusion. I find we are now put upon our last trump; the fox is earthed, but I shall send my two terriers in after him.

SOLDIER
I warrant you, colonel, we'll unkennel him.

LORENZO
And make what haste you can, to bring out the lady.—What say you, father? Burglary is but a venial sin among soldiers.

Father DOMINICK
I shall absolve them, because he is an enemy of the
church.—There is a proverb, I confess, which says, that dead men tell
no tales; but let your soldiers apply it at their own perils.

LORENZO
What, take away a man's wife, and kill him too! The wickedness of this old villain startles me, and gives me a twinge for my own sin, though it comes far short of his.—Hark you, soldiers, be sure you use as little violence to him as is possible.

Father DOMINICK
Hold a little; I have thought better how to secure him, with less danger to us.

LORENZO
O miracle, the friar is grown conscientious!

Father DOMINICK
The old king, you know, is just murdered, and the persons that did it are unknown; let the soldiers seize him for one of the assassinates, and let me alone to accuse him afterwards.

LORENZO
I cry thee mercy with all my heart, for suspecting a friar of the least good nature; what, would you accuse him wrongfully?

Father DOMINICK
I must confess, 'tis wrongful, quoad hoc, as to the fact itself; but 'tis rightful, quoad hunc, as to this heretical rogue, whom we must dispatch. He has railed against the church, which is a fouler crime than the murder of a thousand kings. Omne majus continent in se minus: He, that is an enemy to the church,

is an enemy unto heaven; and he, that is an enemy to heaven, would have killed the king if he had been in the circumstances of doing it; so it is not wrongful to accuse him.

LORENZO
I never knew a churchman, if he were personally offended, but he would bring in heaven by hook or crook into his quarrel.—Soldiers, do as you were first ordered.

[Exeunt **SOLDIERS**.

Father DOMINICK
What was't you ordered them? Are you sure it's safe, and not scandalous?

LORENZO
Somewhat near your own design, but not altogether so mischievous. The people are infinitely discontented, as they have reason; and mutinies there are, or will be, against the queen: now I am content to put him thus far into the plot, that he should be secured as a traitor; but he shall only be prisoner at the soldiers' quarters; and when I am out of reach, he shall be released.

Father DOMINICK
And what will become of me then? for when he is free, he will infallibly accuse me.

LORENZO
Why then, father, you must have recourse to your infallible church-remedies; lie impudently, and swear devoutly, and, as you told me but now, let him try whose oath will be first believed. Retire, I hear them coming.

[They withdraw.

[Enter the **SOLDIERS** with **GOMEZ** struggling on their backs.

GOMEZ
Help, good Christians! help, neighbours! my house is broken open by force, and I am ravished, and like to be assassinated!—What do you mean, villains? will you carry me away, like a pedlar's pack, upon your backs? will you murder a man in plain day-light?

1ST SOLDIER
No; but we'll secure you for a traitor, and for being in a plot against the state.

GOMEZ
Who, I in a plot! O Lord! O Lord! I never durst be in a plot: Why, how can you in conscience suspect a rich citizen of so much wit as to make a plotter? There are none but poor rogues, and those that can't live without it, that are in plots.

2ND SOLDIER
Away with him, away with him.

GOMEZ

O my gold! my wife! my wife! my gold! As I hope to be saved now, I know no more of the plot than they that made it.

[They carry him off, and exeunt.

LORENZO
Thus far we have sailed with a merry gale, and now we have the
Cape of Good Hope in sight; the trade-wind is our own, if we can but
double it.

[He looks out.

[Aside.] Ah, my father and Pedro stand at the corner of the street with company; there's no stirring till they are past.

[Enter **ELVIRA** with a casket.

ELVIRA
Am I come at last into your arms?

LORENZO
Fear nothing; the adventure's ended, and the knight may carry off the lady safely.

ELVIRA
I'm so overjoyed, I can scarce believe I am at liberty; but stand panting, like a bird that has often beaten her wings in vain against her cage, and at last dares hardly venture out, though she sees it open.

Father DOMINICK
Lose no time, but make haste while the way is free for you; and thereupon I give you my benediction.

LORENZO
'Tis not so free as you suppose; for there's an old gentleman of my acquaintance, that blocks up the passage at the corner of the street.

Father DOMINICK
What have you gotten there under your arm, daughter? somewhat, I hope, that will bear your charges in your pilgrimage.

LORENZO
The friar has an hawk's eye to gold and jewels.

ELVIRA
Here's that will make you dance without a fiddle, and provide better entertainment for us, than hedges in summer, and barns in winter. Here's the very heart, and soul, and life-blood of Gomez; pawns in abundance, old gold of widows, and new gold of prodigals, and pearls and diamonds of court ladies, till the next bribe helps their husbands to redeem them.

Father DOMINICK

They are the spoils of the wicked, and the church endows you with them.

LORENZO
And, faith, we'll drink the church's health out of them. But all this while I stand on thorns. Pr'ythee, dear, look out, and see if the coast be free for our escape; for I dare not peep, for fear of being known.

[**ELVIRA** goes to look, and **GOMEZ** comes running in upon her: She shrieks out.

GOMEZ
Thanks to my stars, I have recovered my own territories.—What do I see? I'm ruined! I'm undone! I'm betrayed!

Father DOMINICK [Aside.]
What a hopeful enterprise is here spoiled!

GOMEZ
O, colonel are you there?—and you, friar? nay, then I find how the world goes.

LORENZO
Cheer up, man, thou art out of jeopardy; I heard thee crying out just now, and came running in full speed, with the wings of an eagle, and the feet of a tiger, to thy rescue.

GOMEZ
Ay, you are always at hand to do me a courtesy, with your eagle's feet, and your tiger's wings.—And what were you here for, friar?

Father DOMINICK
To interpose my spiritual authority in your behalf.

GOMEZ
And why did you shriek out, gentlewoman?

ELVIRA
'Twas for joy at your return.

GOMEZ
And that casket under your arm, for what end and purpose?

ELVIRA
Only to preserve it from the thieves.

GOMEZ
And you came running out of doors—

ELVIRA
Only to meet you, sweet husband.

GOMEZ

A fine evidence summed up among you; thank you heartily, you are all my friends. The colonel was walking by accidentally, and hearing my voice, came in to save me; the friar, who was hobbling the same way too, accidentally again, and not knowing of the colonel, I warrant you, he comes in to pray for me; and my faithful wife runs out of doors to meet me, with all my jewels under her arm, and shrieks out for joy at my return. But if my father-in-law had not met your soldiers, colonel, and delivered me in the nick, I should neither have found a friend nor a friar here, and might have shrieked out for joy myself, for the loss of my jewels and my wife.

Father DOMINICK
Art thou an infidel? Wilt thou not believe us?

GOMEZ
Such churchmen as you would make any man an infidel.—Get you into your kennel, gentlewoman; I shall thank you within doors for your safe custody of my jewels and your own.

[He thrusts his **WIFE** off the stage.

As for you, colonel Huffcap, we shall try before a civil magistrate, who's the greater plotter of us two, I against the state, or you against the petticoat.

LORENZO
Nay, if you will complain, you shall for something.

[Beats him.

GOMEZ
Murder, murder! I give up the ghost! I am destroyed! help, murder, murder!

Father DOMINICK
Away, colonel; let us fly for our lives: the neighbours are coming out with forks, and fire-shovels, and spits, and other domestic weapons; the militia of a whole alley is raised against us.

LORENZO
This is but the interest of my debt, master usurer; the principal shall be paid you at our next meeting.

Father DOMINICK
Ah, if your soldiers had but dispatched him, his tongue had been laid asleep, colonel; but this comes of not following good counsel; ah—

[Exeunt **LORENZO** and **FRIAR** severally.

GOMEZ
I'll be revenged of him, if I dare; but he's such a terrible fellow, that my mind misgives me; I shall tremble when I have him before the judge. All my misfortunes come together. I have been robbed, and cuckolded, and ravished, and beaten, in one quarter of an hour; my poor limbs smart, and my poor head aches: ay, do, do, smart limb, ache head, and sprout horns; but I'll be hanged before I'll pity you:—you must needs be married, must ye? there's for that;

[Beats his own head.]

—and to a fine, young, modish lady, must ye? there's for that too; and, at threescore, you old, doting cuckold! take that remembrance;—a fine time of day for a man to be bound prentice, when he is past using of his trade; to set up an equipage of noise, when he has most need of quiet; instead of her being under covert-baron, to be under covert-femme myself; to have my body disabled, and my head fortified; and, lastly, to be crowded into a narrow box with a shrill treble, That with one blast through the whole house does bound, And first taught speaking-trumpets how to sound.

[Exit.

SCENE II.—The Court

Enter **RAYMOND, ALPHONSO,** and **PEDRO**.

RAYMOND
Are these, are these, ye powers, the promised joys,
With which I flattered my long, tedious absence,
To find, at my return, my master murdered?
O, that I could but weep, to vent my passion!
But this dry sorrow burns up all my tears.

ALPHONSO
Mourn inward, brother; 'tis observed at court,
Who weeps, and who wears black; and your return
Will fix all eyes on every act of yours,
To see how you resent King Sancho's death.

RAYMOND
What generous man can live with that constraint
Upon his soul, to bear, much less to flatter,
A court like this! Can I sooth tyranny?
Seem pleased to see my royal master murdered,
His crown usurped, a distaff in the throne,
A council made of such as dare not speak,
And could not, if they durst; whence honest men
Banish themselves, for shame of being there:
A government, that, knowing not true wisdom,
Is scorned abroad, and lives on tricks at home?

ALPHONSO
Virtue must be thrown off; 'tis a coarse garment,
Too heavy for the sun-shine of a court.

RAYMOND
Well then, I will dissemble, for an end

So great, so pious, as a just revenge:
You'll join with me?

ALPHONSO
No honest man but must.

PEDRO
What title has this queen, but lawless force?
And force must pull her down.

ALPHONSO
Truth is, I pity Leonora's case;
Forced, for her safety, to commit a crime,
Which most her soul abhors.

RAYMOND
All she has done, or e'er can do, of good,
This one black deed has damned.

PEDRO
You'll hardly gain your son to our design.

RAYMOND
Your reason for't?

PEDRO
I want time to unriddle it:
Put on your t'other face, the queen approaches.

[Enter **LEONORA**, **BERTRAN**, and **ATTENDANTS**.

RAYMOND
And that accursed Bertran
Stalks close behind her, like a witch's fiend,
Pressing to be employed; stand, and observe them.

LEONORA [to **BERTRAN**]
Buried in private, and so suddenly!
It crosses my design, which was to allow
The rites of funeral fitting his degree,
With all the pomp of mourning.

BERTRAN
It was not safe:
Objects of pity, when the cause is new,
Would work too fiercely on the giddy crowd:
Had Cæsar's body never been exposed,
Brutus had gained his cause.

LEONORA
Then, was he loved?

BERTRAN
O, never man so much, for saint-like goodness.

PEDRO
Had bad men feared him, but as good men loved him,
He had not yet been sainted. [Aside.

LEONORA
I wonder how the people bear his death.

BERTRAN
Some discontents there are; some idle murmurs.

PEDRO
How, idle murmurs! Let me plainly speak:
The doors are all shut up; the wealthier sort,
With arms across, and hats upon their eyes,
Walk to and fro before their silent shops;
Whole droves of lenders crowd the bankers' doors,
To call in money; those, who have none, mark
Where money goes; for when they rise, 'tis plunder:
The rabble gather round the man of news,
And listen with their mouths;
Some tell, some hear, some judge of news, some make it;
And he, who lies most loud, is most believed.

LEONORA
This may be dangerous.

RAYMOND
Pray heaven it may!   [Aside.

BERTRAN
If one of you must fall,
Self-preservation is the first of laws;
And if, when subjects are oppressed by kings,
They justify rebellion by that law,
As well may monarchs turn the edge of right
To cut for them, when self-defence requires it.

LEONORA
You place such arbitrary power in kings,
That I much fear, if I should make you one,
You'll make yourself a tyrant; let these know

By what authority you did this act.

BERTRAN
You much surprise me, to demand that question:
But, since truth must be told, 'twas by your own.

LEONORA
Produce it; or, by heaven, your head shall answer
The forfeit of your tongue.

RAYMOND
Brave mischief towards. [Aside.

BERTRAN
You bade me.

LEONORA
When, and where?

BERTRAN
No, I confess, you bade me not in words;
The dial spoke not, but it made shrewd signs,
And pointed full upon the stroke of murder:
Yet this you said,
You were a woman, ignorant and weak,
So left it to my care.

LEONORA
What, if I said,
I was a woman, ignorant and weak,
Were you to take the advantage of my sex,
And play the devil to tempt me? You contrived,
You urged, you drove me headlong to your toils;
And if, much tired, and frighted more, I paused,
Were you to make my doubts your own commission?

BERTRAN
This 'tis, to serve a prince too faithfully;
Who, free from laws himself, will have that done,
Which, not performed, brings us to sure disgrace;
And, if performed, to ruin.

LEONORA
This 'tis, to counsel things that are unjust;
First, to debauch a king to break his laws,
Which are his safety, and then seek protection
From him you have endangered; but, just heaven,
When sins are judged, will damn the tempting devil,

More deep than those he tempted.

BERTRAN
If princes not protect their ministers,
What man will dare to serve them?

LEONORA
None will dare
To serve them ill, when they are left to laws;
But, when a counsellor, to save himself,
Would lay miscarriages upon his prince,
Exposing him to public rage and hate;
O, 'tis an act as infamously base,
As, should a common soldier sculk behind,
And thrust his general in the front of war:
It shews, he only served himself before,
And had no sense of honour, country, king,
But centered on himself, and used his master,
As guardians do their wards, with shews of care,
But with intent to sell the public safety,
And pocket up his prince.

PEDRO
Well said, i'faith;
This speech is e'en too good for an usurper. [Aside.

BERTRAN
I see for whom I must be sacrificed;
And, had I not been sotted with my zeal,
I might have found it sooner.

LEONORA
From my sight!
The prince, who bears an insolence like this,
Is such an image of the powers above,
As is the statue of the thundering god,
Whose bolts the boys may play with.

BERTRAN
Unrevenged
I will not fall, nor single.

[Exit.

LEONORA
Welcome, welcome! [To **RAYMOND** who kisses her hand.
I saw you not before: One honest lord
Is hid with ease among a crowd of courtiers.

How can I be too grateful to the father
Of such a son as Torrismond?

RAYMOND
His actions were but duty.

LEONORA
Yet, my lord,
All have not paid that debt, like noble Torrismond.
You hear, how Bertran brands me with a crime,
Of which, your son can witness, I am free.
I sent to stop the murder, but too late;
For crimes are swift, but penitence is slow:
The bloody Bertran, diligent in ill,
Flew to prevent the soft returns of pity.

RAYMOND
O cursed haste, of making sure of sin!—
Can you forgive the traitor?

LEONORA
Never, never:
'Tis written here in characters so deep,
That seven years hence, ('till then should I not meet him,)
And in the temple then, I'll drag him thence,
Even from the holy altar to the block.

RAYMOND
She's fired, as I would wish her; aid me, justice,   [Aside.
As all my ends are thine, to gain this point,
And ruin both at once.—It wounds, indeed, [To her.
To bear affronts, too great to be forgiven,
And not have power to punish; yet one way
There is to ruin Bertran.

LEONORA
O, there's none;
Except an host from heaven can make such haste
To save my crown, as he will do to seize it.
You saw, he came surrounded with his friends,
And knew, besides, our army was removed
To quarters too remote for sudden use.

RAYMOND
Yet you may give commission
To some bold man, whose loyalty you trust,
And let him raise the train-bands of the city.

LEONORA
Gross feeders, lion talkers, lamb-like fighters.

RAYMOND
You do not know the virtues of your city,
What pushing force they have; some popular chief,
More noisy than the rest, but cries halloo,
And, in a trice, the bellowing herd come out;
The gates are barred, the ways are barricadoed,
And One and all's the word; true cocks o'the game,
That never ask, for what, or whom, they fight;
But turn them out, and shew them but a foe,
Cry—Liberty! and that's a cause of quarrel.

LEONORA
There may be danger in that boisterous rout:
Who knows, when fires are kindled for my foes,
But some new blast of wind may turn those flames
Against my palace-walls?

RAYMOND
But still their chief
Must be some one, whose loyalty you trust.

LEONORA
And who more proper for that trust than you,
Whose interests, though unknown to you, are mine?
Alphonso, Pedro, haste to raise the rabble;
He shall appear to head them.

RAYMOND [Aside to **ALPHONSO** and **PEDRO**]
First sieze Bertran,
And then insinuate to them, that I bring
Their lawful prince to place upon the throne.

ALPHONSO
Our lawful prince!

RAYMOND
Fear not; I can produce him.

PEDRO [To **ALPHONSO**]
Now we want your son Lorenzo: what a mighty faction
Would he make for us of the city-wives,
With,—Oh, dear husband, my sweet honey husband,
Wont you be for the colonel? if you love me,
Be for the colonel; Oh, he's the finest man!

[Exeunt ALPHONSO and PEDRO.

RAYMOND
So, now we have a plot behind the plot.
She thinks, she's in the depth of my design,
And that 'tis all for her; but time shall show,
She only lives to help me ruin others,
And last, to fall herself. [Aside.

LEONORA
Now, to you, Raymond: can you guess no reason
Why I repose such confidence in you?
You needs must think,
There's some more powerful cause than loyalty:
Will you not speak, to save a lady's blush?
Need I inform you, 'tis for Torrismond,
That all this grace is shown?

RAYMOND
By all the powers, worse, worse than what I feared! [Aside.

LEONORA
And yet, what need I blush at such a choice?
I love a man whom I am proud to love,
And am well pleased my inclination gives
What gratitude would force. O pardon me;
I ne'er was covetous of wealth before;
Yet think so vast a treasure as your son,
Too great for any private man's possession;
And him too rich a jewel, to be set
In vulgar metal, or for vulgar use.

RAYMOND
Arm me with patience, heaven!

LEONORA
How, patience, Raymond?
What exercise of patience have you here?
What find you in my crown to be contemned;
Or in my person loathed? Have I, a queen,
Past by my fellow-rulers of the world,
Whose vying crowns lay glittering in my way,
As if the world were paved with diadems?
Have I refused their blood, to mix with yours,
And raise new kings from so obscure a race,
Fate scarce knew where to find them, when I called?
Have I heaped on my person, crown, and state,
To load the scale, and weighed myself with earth,

For you to spurn the balance?

RAYMOND
Bate the last, and 'tis what I would say:
Can I, can any loyal subject, see
With patience, such a stoop from sovereignty,
An ocean poured upon a narrow brook?
My zeal for you must lay the father by,
And plead my country's cause against my son.
What though his heart be great, his actions gallant,
He wants a crown to poise against a crown,
Birth to match birth, and power to balance power.

LEONORA
All these I have, and these I can bestow;
But he brings worth and virtue to my bed;
And virtue is the wealth which tyrants want:
I stand in need of one, whose glories may
Redeem my crimes, ally me to his fame,
Dispel the factions of my foes on earth,
Disarm the justice of the powers above.

RAYMOND
The people never will endure this choice.

LEONORA
If I endure it, what imports it you?
Go, raise the ministers of my revenge,
Guide with your breath this whirling tempest round,
And see its fury fall where I design.
At last a time for just revenge is given;
Revenge, the darling attribute of heaven:
But man, unlike his Maker, bears too long;
Still more exposed, the more he pardons wrong;
Great in forgiving, and in suffering brave;
To be a saint, he makes himself a slave.

[Exit **QUEEN**.

RAYMOND [Solus.]
Marriage with Torrismond! it must not be,
By heaven, it must not be! or, if it be,
Law, justice, honour, bid farewell to earth,
For heaven leaves all to tyrants.

[Enter **TORRISMOND**, who kneels to him.

TORRISMOND

O, very welcome, sir!
But doubly now! You come in such a time,
As if propitious fortune took a care,
To swell my tide of joys to their full height,
And leave me nothing farther to desire.

RAYMOND
I hope, I come in time, if not to make,
At least to save your fortune and your honour.
Take heed you steer your vessel right, my son;
This calm of heaven, this mermaid's melody,
Into an unseen whirlpool draws you fast,
And, in a moment, sinks you.

TORRISMOND
Fortune cannot,
And fate can scarce; I've made the port already,
And laugh securely at the lazy storm,
That wanted wings to reach me in the deep.
Your pardon, sir; my duty calls me hence;
I go to find my queen, my earthly goddess,
To whom I owe my hopes, my life, my love.

RAYMOND
You owe her more, perhaps, than you imagine;
Stay, I command you stay, and hear me first.
This hour's the very crisis of your fate,
Your good or ill, your infamy or fame,
And all the colour of your life, depends
On this important now.

TORRISMOND
I see no danger;
The city, army, court, espouse my cause,
And, more than all, the queen, with public favour,
Indulges my pretensions to her love.

RAYMOND
Nay, if possessing her can make you happy,
'Tis granted, nothing hinders your design.

TORRISMOND
If she can make me blest? she only can;
Empire, and wealth, and all she brings beside,
Are but the train and trappings of her love:
The sweetest, kindest, truest of her sex,
In whose possession years roll round on years,
And joys, in circles, meet new joys again;

Kisses, embraces, languishing, and death,
Still from each other to each other move,
To crown the various seasons of our love;
And doubt you if such love can make me happy?

RAYMOND
Yes; for, I think, you love your honour more.

TORRISMOND
And what can shock my honour in a queen?

RAYMOND
A tyrant, an usurper?

TORRISMOND
Grant she be;
When from the conqueror we hold our lives,
We yield ourselves his subjects from that hour;
For mutual benefits make mutual ties.

RAYMOND
Why, can you think I owe a thief my life,
Because he took it not by lawless force?
What, if he did not all the ill he could?
Am I obliged by that to assist his rapines,
And to maintain his murders?

TORRISMOND
Not to maintain, but bear them unrevenged.
Kings' titles commonly begin by force,
Which time wears off, and mellows into right;
So power, which, in one age, is tyranny,
Is ripened, in the next, to true succession:
She's in possession.

RAYMOND
So diseases are:
Should not a lingering fever be removed,
Because it long has raged within my blood?
Do I rebel, when I would thrust it out?
What, shall I think the world was made for one,
And men are born for kings, as beasts for men,
Not for protection, but to be devoured?
Mark those, who dote on arbitrary power,
And you shall find them either hot-brained youth,
Or needy bankrupts, servile in their greatness,
And slaves to some, to lord it o'er the rest.
O baseness, to support a tyrant throne,

And crush your freeborn brethren of the world!
Nay, to become a part of usurpation;
To espouse the tyrant's person and her crimes,
And, on a tyrant, get a race of tyrants,
To be your country's curse in after ages.

TORRISMOND
I see no crime in her whom I adore,
Or, if I do, her beauty makes it none:
Look on me as a man abandoned o'er
To an eternal lethargy of love;
To pull, and pinch, and wound me, cannot cure,
And but disturb the quiet of my death.

RAYMOND
O virtue, virtue! what art thou become,
That man should leave thee for that toy, a woman,
Made from the dross and refuse of a man!
Heaven took him, sleeping, when he made her too;
Had man been waking, he had ne'er consented.
Now, son, suppose
Some brave conspiracy were ready formed,
To punish tyrants, and redeem the land,
Could you so far belie your country's hope,
As not to head the party?

TORRISMOND
How could my hand rebel against my heart?

RAYMOND
How could your heart rebel against your reason?

TORRISMOND
No honour bids me fight against myself;
The royal family is all extinct,
And she, who reigns, bestows her crown on me:
So must I be ungrateful to the living,
To be but vainly pious to the dead,
While you defraud your offspring of their fate.

RAYMOND
Mark who defraud their offspring, you or I?
For know, there yet survives the lawful heir
Of Sancho's blood, whom when I shall produce,
I rest assured to see you pale with fear,
And trembling at his name.

TORRISMOND

He must be more than man, who makes me tremble.
I dare him to the field, with all the odds
Of justice on his side, against my tyrant:
Produce your lawful prince, and you shall see
How brave a rebel love has made your son.

RAYMOND
Read that; 'tis with the royal signet signed,
And given me, by the king, when time should serve,
To be perused by you.

TORRISMOND [Reads.]
I, the king.
My youngest and alone surviving son,
Reported dead, to escape rebellious rage,
Till happier times shall call his courage forth,
To break my fetters, or revenge my fate,
I will that Raymond educate as his,
And call him Torrismond—
If I am he, that son, that Torrismond,
The world contains not so forlorn a wretch!
Let never man believe he can be happy!
For, when I thought my fortune most secure,
One fatal moment tears me from my joys;
And when two hearts were joined by mutual love,
The sword of justice cuts upon the knot,
And severs them for ever.

RAYMOND
True, it must.

TORRISMOND
O, cruel man, to tell me that it must!
If you have any pity in your breast,
Redeem me from this labyrinth of fate,
And plunge me in my first obscurity.
The secret is alone between us two;
And, though you would not hide me from myself,
O, yet be kind, conceal me from the world,
And be my father still!

RAYMOND
Your lot's too glorious, and the proof's too plain.
Now, in the name of honour, sir, I beg you,—
Since I must use authority no more,—
On these old knees, I beg you, ere I die,
That I may see your father's death revenged.

TORRISMOND
Why, 'tis the only business of my life;
My order's issued to recall the army,
And Bertran's death's resolved.

RAYMOND
And not the queen's? O, she's the chief offender!
Shall justice turn her edge within your hand?
No, if she 'scape, you are yourself the tyrant,
And murderer of your father.

TORRISMOND
Cruel fates!
To what have you reserved me?

RAYMOND
Why that sigh?

TORRISMOND
Since you must know,—but break, O break, my heart,
Before I tell my fatal story out!—
The usurper of my throne, my house's ruin!
The murderer of my father,—is my wife!

RAYMOND
O horror, horror!—After this alliance,
Let tigers match with hinds, and wolves with sheep,
And every creature couple with his foe.
How vainly man designs, when heaven opposes!
I bred you up to arms, raised you to power,
Permitted you to fight for this usurper,
Indeed to save a crown, not hers, but yours,
All to make sure the vengeance of this day,
Which even this day has ruined. One more question
Let me but ask, and I have done for ever;—
Do you yet love the cause of all your woes,
Or is she grown, as sure she ought to be,
More odious to your sight than toads and adders?

TORRISMOND
O there's the utmost malice of my fate,
That I am bound to hate, and born to love!

RAYMOND
No more!—Farewell, my much lamented king!—
I dare not trust him with himself so far,
To own him to the people as their king,
Before their rage has finished my designs

On Bertran and the queen; but in despite,
Even of himself, I'll save him.

[Aside and exit.

TORRISMOND
'Tis but a moment since I have been king,
And weary on't already; I'm a lover,
And loved, possess,—yet all these make me wretched;
And heaven has given me blessings for a curse.
With what a load of vengeance am I prest,
Yet, never, never, can I hope for rest;
For when my heavy burden I remove,
The weight falls down, and crushes her I love.

[Exit.

ACT V

SCENE I.—A Bed-Chamber

Enter **TORRISMOND**.

TORRISMOND
Love, justice, nature, pity, and revenge,
Have kindled up a wildfire in my breast,
And I am all a civil war within!

[Enter **QUEEN** and **TERESA**, at a distance.

My Leonora there!—
Mine! is she mine? my father's murderer mine?
O! that I could, with honour, love her more,
Or hate her less, with reason!—See, she weeps!
Thinks me unkind, or false, and knows not why
I thus estrange my person from her bed!
Shall I not tell her?—no; 'twill break her heart;
She'll know too soon her own and my misfortunes.

[Exit.

LEONORA
He's gone, and I am lost; did'st thou not see
His sullen eyes? how gloomily they glanced?
He looked not like the Torrismond I loved.

TERESA
Can you not guess from whence this change proceeds?

LEONORA
No: there's the grief, Teresa: Oh, Teresa!
Fain would I tell thee what I feel within,
But shame and modesty have tied my tongue!
Yet, I will tell, that thou may'st weep with me.—
How dear, how sweet his first embraces were!
With what a zeal he joined his lips to mine!
And sucked my breath at every word I spoke,
As if he drew his inspiration hence:
While both our souls came upward to our mouths,
As neighbouring monarchs at their borders meet;
I thought—Oh, no; 'tis false! I could not think;
'Twas neither life nor death, but both in one.

TERESA
Then, sure his transports were not less than yours.

LEONORA
More, more! for, by the high-hung tapers' light,
I could discern his cheeks were glowing red,
His very eyeballs trembled with his love,
And sparkled through their casements humid fires;
He sighed, and kissed; breathed short, and would have spoke,
But was too fierce to throw away the time;
All he could say was—love and Leonora.

TERESA
How then can you suspect him lost so soon?

LEONORA
Last night he flew not with a bridegroom's haste,
Which eagerly prevents the appointed hour:
I told the clocks, and watched the wasting light,
And listened to each softly-treading step,
In hope 'twas he; but still it was not he.
At last he came, but with such altered looks,
So wild, so ghastly, as if some ghost had met him:
All pale, and speechless, he surveyed me round;
Then, with a groan, he threw himself a-bed,
But, far from me, as far as he could move,
And sighed and tossed, and turned, but still from me.

TERESA
What, all the night?

LEONORA
Even all the livelong night.
At last, (for, blushing, I must tell thee all,)
I pressed his hand, and laid me by his side;
He pulled it back, as if he touched a serpent.
With that I burst into a flood of tears,
And asked him how I had offended him?
He answered nothing, but with sighs and groans;
So, restless, past the night; and, at the dawn,
Leapt from the bed, and vanished.

TERESA
Sighs and groans,
Paleness and trembling, all are signs of love;
He only fears to make you share his sorrows.

LEONORA
I wish 'twere so; but love still doubts the worst;
My heavy heart, the prophetess of woes,
Forebodes some ill at hand: to sooth my sadness,
Sing me the song, which poor Olympia made,
When false Bireno left her.

SONG.

Farewell, ungrateful traitor!
Farewell, my perjured swain!
Let never injured creature
Believe a man again.
The pleasure of possessing
Surpasses all expressing,
But 'tis too short a blessing,
And love too long a pain.

'Tis easy to deceive us,
In pity of your pain;
But when we love, you leave us,
To rail at you in vain.
Before we have descried it,
There is no bliss beside it;
But she, that once has tried it,
Will never love again.

The passion you pretended,
Was only to obtain;
But when the charm is ended,
The charmer you disdain.
Your love by ours we measure,

Till we have lost our treasure;
But dying is a pleasure,
When living is a pain.

[Re-enter **TORRISMOND**.

TORRISMOND
Still she is here, and still I cannot speak;
But wander, like some discontented ghost,
That oft appears, but is forbid to talk.

[Going again.

LEONORA
O, Torrismond, if you resolve my death,
You need no more, but to go hence again;
Will you not speak?

TORRISMOND
I cannot.

LEONORA
Speak! oh, speak!
Your anger would be kinder than your silence.

TORRISMOND
Oh!—

LEONORA
Do not sigh, or tell me why you sigh.

TORRISMOND
Why do I live, ye powers!

LEONORA
Why do I live to hear you speak that word?
Some black-mouthed villain has defamed my virtue.

TORRISMOND
No, no! Pray, let me go.

LEONORA [Kneeling.]
You shall not go!
By all the pleasures of our nuptial bed,
If ever I was loved, though now I'm not,
By these true tears, which, from my wounded heart,
Bleed at my eyes—

TORRISMOND
Rise.

LEONORA
I will never rise;
I cannot chuse a better place to die.

TORRISMOND
Oh! I would speak, but cannot.

LEONORA [Rising.]
Guilt keeps you silent then; you love me not:
What have I done, ye powers, what have I done,
To see my youth, my beauty, and my love,
No sooner gained, but slighted and betrayed;
And, like a rose, just gathered from the stalk,
But only smelt, and cheaply thrown aside,
To wither on the ground.

TERESA
For heaven's sake, madam, moderate your passion!

LEONORA
Why namest thou heaven? there is no heaven for me.
Despair, death, hell, have seized my tortured soul!
When I had raised his grovelling fate from ground,
To power and love, to empire, and to me;
When each embrace was dearer than the first;
Then, then to be contemned; then, then thrown off!
It calls me old, and withered, and deformed,
And loathsome! Oh! what woman can bear loathsome?
The turtle flies not from his billing mate,
He bills the closer; but, ungrateful man,
Base, barbarous man! the more we raise our love,
The more we pall, and kill, and cool his ardour.
Racks, poison, daggers, rid me of my life;
And any death is welcome.

TORRISMOND
Be witness all ye powers, that know my heart,
I would have kept the fatal secret hid;
But she has conquered, to her ruin conquered:
Here, take this paper, read our destinies;—
Yet do not; but, in kindness to yourself,
Be ignorantly safe.

LEONORA
No! give it me,

Even though it be the sentence of my death.

TORRISMOND
Then see how much unhappy love has made us.
O Leonora! Oh!
We two were born when sullen planets reigned;
When each the other's influence opposed,
And drew the stars to factions at our birth.
Oh! better, better had it been for us,
That we had never seen, or never loved.

LEONORA
There is no faith in heaven, if heaven says so;
You dare not give it.

TORRISMOND
As unwillingly,
As I would reach out opium to a friend,
Who lay in torture, and desired to die.

[Gives the Paper.

But now you have it, spare my sight the pain
Of seeing what a world of tears it costs you.
Go, silently, enjoy your part of grief,
And share the sad inheritance with me.

LEONORA
I have a thirsty fever in my soul;
Give me but present ease, and let me die.

[Exeunt **QUEEN** and **TERESA**.

[Enter **LORENZO**.

LORENZO
Arm, arm, my lord! the city bands are up;
Drums beating, colours flying, shouts confused;
All clustering in a heap, like swarming hives,
And rising in a moment.

TORRISMOND
With design to punish Bertran, and revenge the king;
'Twas ordered so.

LORENZO
Then you're betrayed, my lord.
'Tis true, they block the castle kept by Bertran,

But now they cry, "Down with the palace, fire it,
Pull out the usurping queen!"

TORRISMOND
The queen, Lorenzo! durst they name the queen?

LORENZO
If railing and reproaching be to name her.

TORRISMOND
O sacrilege! say quickly, who commands
This vile blaspheming rout?

LORENZO
I'm loth to tell you;
But both our fathers thrust them headlong on,
And bear down all before them.

TORRISMOND
Death and hell!
Somewhat must be resolved, and speedily.
How say'st thou, my Lorenzo? dar'st thou be
A friend, and once forget thou art a son,
To help me save the queen?

LORENZO [Aside.]
Let me consider:—
Bear arms against my father? he begat me;—
That's true; but for whose sake did he beget me?
For his own, sure enough: for me he knew not.
Oh! but says conscience,—Fly in nature's face?—
But how, if nature fly in my face first?
Then nature's the aggressor; let her look to't.—
He gave me life, and he may take it back:
No, that's boys' play, say I.
'Tis policy for a son and father to take different sides:
For then, lands and tenements commit no treason.
[To **TORRISMOND**] Sir, upon mature consideration, I have found my father to be little better than a rebel, and therefore, I'll do my best to secure him, for your sake; in hope, you may secure him hereafter for my sake.

TORRISMOND
Put on thy utmost speed to head the troops,
Which every moment I expect to arrive;
Proclaim me, as I am, the lawful king:
I need not caution thee for Raymond's life,
Though I no more must call him father now.

LORENZO [Aside.]
How! not call him father? I see preferment alters a man strangely; this may serve me for a use of instruction, to cast off my father when I am great. Methought too, he called himself the lawful king; intimating sweetly, that he knows what's what with our sovereign lady:—Well if I rout my father, as I hope in heaven I shall, I am in a fair way to be the prince of the blood.—Farewell, general; I will bring up those that shall try what mettle there is in orange tawny.

[Exit.

TORRISMOND [At the Door.]
Haste there; command the guards be all drawn up
Before the palace-gate.—By heaven, I'll face
This tempest, and deserve the name of king!
O Leonora, beauteous in thy crimes,
Never were hell and heaven so matched before!
Look upward, fair, but as thou look'st on me;
Then all the blest will beg, that thou may'st live,
And even my father's ghost his death forgive.

[Exit.

SCENE II.—The Palace-Yard. Drums and Trumpets Within

Enter **RAYMOND, ALPHONSO, PEDRO,** and their **PARTY.**

RAYMOND
Now, valiant citizens, the time is come,
To show your courage, and your loyalty.
You have a prince of Sancho's royal blood,
The darling of the heavens, and joy of earth;
When he's produced, as soon he shall, among you,
Speak, what will you adventure to reseat him
Upon his father's throne?

OMNES
Our lives and fortunes.

RAYMOND
What then remains to perfect our success;
But o'er the tyrant's guards to force our way?

OMNES
Lead on, lead on.

[Drums and Trumpets on the other side.

[Enter **TORRISMOND** and his **PARTY**: As they are going to fight, he speaks.

TORRISMOND [To his.]
Hold, hold your arms.

RAYMOND [To his.]
Retire.

ALPHONSO
What means this pause?

PEDRO
Peace; nature works within them.

[**ALPHONSO** and **PEDRO** go apart.

TORRISMOND
How comes it, good old man, that we two meet
On these harsh terms? thou very reverend rebel;
Thou venerable traitor, in whose face
And hoary hairs treason is sanctified,
And sin's black dye seems blanched by age to virtue.

RAYMOND
What treason is it to redeem my king,
And to reform the state?

TORRISMOND
That's a stale cheat;
The primitive rebel, Lucifer, first used it,
And was the first reformer of the skies.

RAYMOND
What, if I see my prince mistake a poison,
Call it a cordial,—am I then a traitor,
Because I hold his hand, or break the glass?

TORRISMOND
How darest thou serve thy king against his will?

RAYMOND
Because 'tis then the only time to serve him.

TORRISMOND
I take the blame of all upon myself;
Discharge thy weight on me.

RAYMOND

O never, never!
Why, 'tis to leave a ship, tossed in a tempest,
Without the pilot's care.

TORRISMOND
I'll punish thee;
By heaven, I will, as I would punish rebels,
Thou stubborn loyal man!

RAYMOND
First let me see
Her punished, who misleads you from your fame;
Then burn me, hack me, hew me into pieces,
And I shall die well pleased.

TORRISMOND
Proclaim my title,
To save the effusion of my subjects' blood; and thou shalt still
Be as my foster-father near my breast,
And next my Leonora.

RAYMOND
That word stabs me.
You shall be still plain Torrismond with me;
The abettor, partner, (if you like that name,)
The husband of a tyrant; but no king,
Till you deserve that title by your justice.

TORRISMOND
Then farewell, pity; I will be obeyed.—
[To the **PEOPLE**] Hear, you mistaken men, whose loyalty
Runs headlong into treason: See your prince!
In me behold your murdered Sancho's son;
Dismiss your arms, and I forgive your crimes.

RAYMOND
Believe him not; he raves; his words are loose
As heaps of sand, and scattering wide from sense.
You see he knows not me, his natural father;
But, aiming to possess the usurping queen,
So high he's mounted in his airy hopes,
That now the wind is got into his head,
And turns his brains to frenzy.

TORRISMOND
Hear me yet; I am—

RAYMOND

Fall on, fall on, and hear him not;
But spare his person, for his father's sake.

PEDRO
Let me come; if he be mad, I have that shall cure him. There's no surgeon in all Arragon has so much dexterity as I have at breathing of the temple-vein.

TORRISMOND
My right for me!

RAYMOND
Our liberty for us!

OMNES
Liberty, liberty!

[As they are ready to Fight, enter **LORENZO** and his **PARTY**.

LORENZO
On forfeit of your lives, lay down your arms.

ALPHONSO
How, rebel, art thou there?

LORENZO
Take your rebel back again, father mine: The beaten party are rebels to the conquerors. I have been at hard-head with your butting citizens; I have routed your herd; I have dispersed them; and now they are retreated quietly, from their extraordinary vocation of fighting in the streets, to their ordinary vocation of cozening in their shops.

TORRISMOND [To **RAYMOND**]
You see 'tis vain contending with the truth;
Acknowledge what I am.

RAYMOND
You are my king;—would you would be your own!
But, by a fatal fondness, you betray
Your fame and glory to the usurper's bed.
Enjoy the fruits of blood and parricide,
Take your own crown from Leonora's gift,
And hug your father's murderer in your arms!

[Enter **QUEEN**, **TERESA**, and **WOMEN**.

ALPHONSO
No more; behold the queen.

RAYMOND

Behold the basilisk of Torrismond,
That kills him with her eyes—I will speak on;
My life is of no farther use to me:
I would have chaffered it before for vengeance;
Now let it go for failing.

TORRISMOND
My heart sinks in me while I hear him speak,
And every slackened fibre drops its hold,
Like nature letting down the springs of life;
So much the name of father awes me still—[Aside.
Send off the crowd; for you, now I have conquered,
I can hear with honour your demands.

LORENZO [To **ALPHONSO**]
Now, sir, who proves the traitor? My conscience is true to me; it always whispers right, when I have my regiment to back it.

[Exeunt **LORENZO, ALPHONSO, PEDRO** &c.

TORRISMOND
O Leonora, what can love do more?
I have opposed your ill fate to the utmost;
Combated heaven and earth to keep you mine;
And yet at last that tyrant justice! Oh—

LEONORA
'Tis past, 'tis past, and love is ours no more;
Yet I complain not of the powers above;
They made me a miser's feast of happiness,
And could not furnish out another meal.
Now, by yon stars, by heaven, and earth, and men,
By all my foes at once, I swear, my Torrismond,
That to have had you mine for one short day,
Has cancelled half my mighty sum of woes!
Say but you hate me not.

TORRISMOND
I cannot hate you.

RAYMOND
Can you not? say that once more,
That all the saints may witness it against you.

LEONORA
Cruel Raymond!
Can he not punish me, but he must hate?
O, 'tis not justice, but a brutal rage,

Which hates the offender's person with his crimes!
I have enough to overwhelm one woman,
To lose a crown and lover in a day:
Let pity lend a tear, when rigour strikes.

RAYMOND
Then, then you should have thought of tears and pity,
When virtue, majesty, and hoary age,
Pleaded for Sancho's life.

LEONORA
My future days shall be one whole contrition:
A chapel will I build, with large endowment,
Where every day an hundred aged men
Shall all hold up their withered hands to heaven,
To pardon Sancho's death.

TORRISMOND
See, Raymond, see; she makes a large amends:
Sancho is dead; no punishment of her
Can raise his cold stiff limbs from the dark grave;
Nor can his blessed soul look down from heaven,
Or break the eternal sabbath of his rest,
To see, with joy, her miseries on earth.

RAYMOND
Heaven may forgive a crime to penitence,
For heaven can judge if penitence be true;
But man, who knows not hearts, should make examples
Which, like a warning piece, must be shot off,
To fright the rest from crimes.

LEONORA
Had I but known that Sancho was his father,
I would have poured a deluge of my blood,
To save one drop of his.

TORRISMOND
Mark that, inexorable Raymond, mark!
'Twas fatal ignorance, that caused his death.

RAYMOND
What! if she did not know he was your father,
She knew he was a man, the best of men;
Heaven's image double-stamped, as man and king.

LEONORA
He was, he was, even more than you can say;

But yet—

RAYMOND
But yet you barbarously murdered him.

LEONORA
He will not hear me out!

TORRISMOND
Was ever criminal forbid to plead?
Curb your ill-mannered zeal.

RAYMOND
Sing to him, syren;
For I shall stop my ears: Now mince the sin,
And mollify damnation with a phrase;
Say, you consented not to Sancho's death,
But barely not forbade it.

LEONORA
Hard-hearted man, I yield my guilty cause;
But all my guilt was caused by too much love.
Had I, for jealousy of empire, sought
Good Sancho's death, Sancho had died before.
'Twas always in my power to take his life;
But interest never could my conscience blind,
Till love had cast a mist before my eyes,
And made me think his death the only means
Which could secure my throne to Torrismond.

TORRISMOND
Never was fatal mischief meant so kind,
For all she gave has taken all away.
Malicious powers! is this to be restored?
'Tis to be worse deposed than Sancho was.

RAYMOND
Heaven has restored you, you depose yourself.
Oh, when young kings begin with scorn of justice,
They make an omen to their after reign,
And blot their annals in the foremost page.

TORRISMOND
No more; lest you be made the first example,
To show how I can punish.

RAYMOND
Once again:

Let her be made your father's sacrifice,
And after make me hers.

TORRISMOND
Condemn a wife!
That were to atone for parricide with murder.

RAYMOND
Then let her be divorced: we'll be content
With that poor scanty justice; let her part.

TORRISMOND
Divorce! that's worse than death, 'tis death of love.

LEONORA
The soul and body part not with such pain,
As I from you; but yet 'tis just, my lord:
I am the accurst of heaven, the hate of earth,
Your subjects' detestation, and your ruin;
And therefore fix this doom upon myself.

TORRISMOND
Heaven! Can you wish it, to be mine no more?

LEONORA
Yes, I can wish it, as the dearest proof,
And last, that I can make you of my love.
To leave you blest, I would be more accurst
Than death can make me; for death ends our woes,
And the kind grave shuts up the mournful scene:
But I would live without you, to be wretched long;
And hoard up every moment of my life,
To lengthen out the payment of my tears,
Till even fierce Raymond, at the last, shall say,—
Now let her die, for she has grieved enough.

TORRISMOND
Hear this, hear this, thou tribune of the people!
Thou zealous, public blood-hound, hear, and melt!

RAYMOND [Aside.]
I could cry now; my eyes grow womanish,
But yet my heart holds out.

LEONORA
Some solitary cloister will I chuse,
And there with holy virgins live immured:
Coarse my attire, and short shall be my sleep,

Broke by the melancholy midnight bell.
Now, Raymond, now be satisfied at last:
Fasting and tears, and penitence and prayer,
Shall do dead Sancho justice every hour.

RAYMOND [Aside.]
By your leave, manhood!

[Wipes his eyes.

TORRISMOND
He weeps! now he is vanquished.

RAYMOND
No: 'tis a salt rheum, that scalds my eyes.

LEONORA
If he were vanquished, I am still unconquered.
I'll leave you in the height of all my love,
Even when my heart is beating out its way,
And struggles to you most.
Farewell, a last farewell, my dear, dear lord!
Remember me!—speak, Raymond, will you let him?
Shall he remember Leonora's love,
And shed a parting tear to her misfortunes?

RAYMOND [Almost crying.]
Yes, yes, he shall; pray go.

TORRISMOND
Now, by my soul, she shall not go: why, Raymond,
Her every tear is worth a father's life.
Come to my arms, come, my fair penitent!
Let us not think what future ills may fall.
But drink deep draughts of love, and lose them all.

[Exeunt **TORRISMOND** with the **QUEEN**.

RAYMOND
No matter yet, he has my hook within him.
Now let him frisk and flounce, and run and roll,
And think to break his hold; he toils in vain.
This love, the bait he gorged so greedily,
Will make him sick, and then I have him sure.

[Enter **ALPHONSO** and **PEDRO**.

ALPHONSO

Brother, there's news from Bertran; he desires
Admittance to the king, and cries aloud,—
This day shall end our fears of civil war!—
For his safe conduct he entreats your presence,
And begs you would be speedy.

RAYMOND
Though I loath
The traitor's sight, I'll go. Attend us here.

[Exit.

[Enter **GOMEZ, ELVIRA, Father DOMINICK**, with **OFFICERS**, to make the Stage as full as possible.

PEDRO
Why, how now, Gomez? what mak'st thou here, with a whole brotherhood of city-bailiffs? Why, thou look'st like Adam in Paradise, with his guard of beasts about him.

GOMEZ
Ay, and a man had need of them, Don Pedro; for here are the two old seducers, a wife and priest,—that's Eve and the serpent,—at my elbow.

Father DOMINICK
Take notice how uncharitably he talks of churchmen.

GOMEZ
Indeed, you are a charitable belswagger! My wife cried out,—"Fire, fire!" and you brought out your church-buckets, and called for engines to play against it.

ALPHONSO
I am sorry you are come hither to accuse your wife; her education has been virtuous, her nature mild and easy.

GOMEZ
Yes! she's easy, with a vengeance; there's a certain colonel has found her so.

ALPHONSO
She came a spotless virgin to your bed.

GOMEZ
And she's a spotless virgin still for me—she's never the worse for my wearing, I'll take my oath on't. I have lived with her with all the innocence of a man of threescore, like a peaceable bed-fellow as I am.

ELVIRA
Indeed, sir, I have no reason to complain of him for disturbing of my sleep.

Father DOMINICK
A fine commendation you have given yourself; the church did not marry you for that.

PEDRO
Come, come, your grievances, your grievances.

Father DOMINICK
Why, noble sir, I'll tell you.

GOMEZ
Peace, friar! and let me speak first. I am the plaintiff. Sure you think you are in the pulpit, where you preach by hours.

Father DOMINICK
And you edify by minutes.

GOMEZ
Where you make doctrines for the people, and uses and applications for yourselves.

PEDRO
Gomez, give way to the old gentleman in black.

GOMEZ
No! the t'other old gentleman in black shall take me if I do; I will speak first!—Nay, I will, friar, for all your verbum sacerdotis. I'll speak truth in few words, and then you may come afterwards and lie by the clock as you use to do.—For, let me tell you, gentlemen, he shall lie and forswear himself with any friar in all Spain; that's a bold word now.—

Father DOMINICK
Let him alone; let him alone; I shall fetch him back with a circum-bendibus, I warrant him.

ALPHONSO
Well, what have you to say against your wife, Gomez?

GOMEZ
Why, I say, in the first place, that I and all men are married for our sins, and that our wives are a judgment; that a batchelor-cobler is a happier man than a prince in wedlock; that we are all visited with a household plague, and, Lord have mercy upon us should be written on all our doors[2].

Father DOMINICK
Now he reviles marriage, which is one of the seven blessed sacraments.

GOMEZ
'Tis liker one of the seven deadly sins: but make your best on't, I care not; 'tis but binding a man neck and heels, for all that. But, as for my wife, that crocodile of Nilus, she has wickedly and traitorously conspired the cuckoldom of me, her anointed sovereign lord; and, with the help of the aforesaid friar, whom heaven confound, and with the limbs of one colonel Hernando, cuckold-maker of this city, devilishly contrived to steal herself away, and under her arm feloniously to bear one casket of diamonds, pearls, and other jewels, to the value of 30,000 pistoles.—Guilty, or not guilty? how sayest thou, culprit?

Father DOMINICK
False and scandalous! Give me the book. I'll take my corporal oath point-blank against every particular of this charge.

ELVIRA
And so will I.

Father DOMINICK
As I was walking in the streets, telling my beads, and praying to myself, according to my usual custom, I heard a foul out-cry before Gomez' portal; and his wife, my penitent, making doleful lamentations: thereupon, making what haste my limbs would suffer me, that are crippled with often kneeling, I saw him spurning and listing her most unmercifully; whereupon, using Christian arguments with him to desist, he fell violently upon me, without respect to my sacerdotal orders, pushed me from him, and turned me about with a finger and a thumb, just as a man would set up a top. Mercy! quoth I.—Damme! quoth he;—and still continued labouring me, until a good-minded colonel came by, whom, as heaven shall save me, I had never seen before.

GOMEZ
O Lord! O Lord!

Father DOMINICK
Ay, and O lady! O lady too!—I redouble my oath, I had never seen him. Well, this noble colonel, like a true gentleman, was for taking the weaker part, you may be sure; whereupon this Gomez flew upon him like a dragon, got him down, the devil being strong in him, and gave him bastinado upon bastinado, and buffet upon buffet, which the poor meek colonel, being prostrate, suffered with a most Christian patience.

GOMEZ
Who? he meek? I'm sure I quake at the very thought of him; why, he's as fierce as Rhodomont; he made assault and battery upon my person, beat me into all the colours of the rainbow; and every word this abominable priest has uttered is as false as the Alcoran. But if you want a thorough-paced liar, that will swear through thick and thin, commend me to a friar.

[Enter **LORENZO**, who comes behind the **COMPANY**, and stands at his **FATHERS** back unseen, over-against **GOMEZ**.

LORENZO
How now! What's here to do? my cause a trying, as I live, and that before my own father.—Now fourscore take him for an old bawdy magistrate, that stands like the picture of madam Justice, with a pair of scales in his hand, to weigh lechery by ounces! [Aside.

ALPHONSO
Well—but all this while, who is this colonel Hernando?

GOMEZ
He's the first begotten of Beelzebub, with a face as terrible as Demogorgon.

[**LORENZO** peeps over **ALPHONSO'S** Head, and stares at **GOMEZ**.

No! I lie, I lie. He's a very proper handsome fellow! well proportioned, and clean shaped, with a face like a cherubin.

PEDRO
What, backward and forward, Gomez! dost thou hunt counter?

ALPHONSO
Had this colonel any former design upon your wife? for, if that be proved, you shall have justice.

GOMEZ [Aside.]
Now I dare speak,—let him look as dreadfully as he will.—I say, sir, and I will prove it, that he had a lewd design upon her body, and attempted to corrupt her honesty.

[**LORENZO** lifts up his fist clenched at him.

I confess my wife was as willing—as himself; and, I believe, 'twas she corrupted him; for I have known him formerly a very civil and modest person.

ELVIRA
You see, sir, he contradicts himself at every word; he's plainly mad.

ALPHONSO
Speak boldly, man! and say what thou wilt stand by: did he strike thee?

GOMEZ
I will speak boldly; he struck me on the face before my own threshold, that the very walls cried shame to him.

[**LORENZO** holds up again.

'Tis true, I gave him provocation, for the man's as peaceable a gentleman as any is in all Spain.

Father DOMINICK
Now the truth comes out, in spite of him.

PEDRO
I believe the friar has bewitched him.

ALPHONSO
For my part, I see no wrong that has been offered him.

GOMEZ
How? no wrong? why, he ravished me, with the help of two soldiers, carried me away vi et armis, and would put me into a plot against government.

[**LORENZO** holds up again.

I confess, I never could endure the government, because it was tyrannical; but my sides and shoulders are black and blue, as I can strip and show the marks of them.

[**LORENZO** again.

But that might happen, too, by a fall that I got yesterday upon the pebbles.

[All laugh.

Father DOMINICK
Fresh straw, and a dark chamber; a most manifest judgment! there never comes better of railing against the church.

GOMEZ
Why, what will you have me say? I think you'll make me mad: truth has been at my tongue's end this half hour, and I have not power to bring it out, for fear of this bloody-minded colonel.

ALPHONSO
What colonel?

GOMEZ
Why, my colonel—I mean my wife's colonel, that appears there to me like my malus genius, terrifies me.

ALPHONSO [Turning.]
Now you are mad indeed, Gomez; this is my son Lorenzo.

GOMEZ
How? your son Lorenzo! it is impossible.

ALPHONSO
As true as your wife Elvira is my daughter.

LORENZO
What, have I taken all this pains about a sister?

GOMEZ
No, you have taken some about me; I am sure, if you are her brother, my sides can show the tokens of our alliance.

ALPHONSO [to **LORENZO**]
You know I put your sister into a nunnery, with a strict command not to see you, for fear you should have wrought upon her to have taken the habit, which was never my intention; and consequently, I married her without your knowledge, that it might not be in your power to prevent it.

ELVIRA
You see, brother, I had a natural affection to you.

LORENZO

What a delicious harlot have I lost! Now, pox upon me, for being so near a-kin to thee!

ELVIRA
However, we are both beholden to friar Dominick; the church is an indulgent mother, she never fails to do her part.

Father DOMINICK
Heavens! what will become of me?

GOMEZ
Why, you are not like to trouble heaven; those fat guts were never made for mounting.

LORENZO
I shall make bold to disburden him of my hundred pistoles, to make him the lighter for his journey: indeed, 'tis partly out of conscience, that I may not be accessory to his breaking his vow of poverty.

ALPHONSO
I have no secular power to reward the pains you have taken with my daughter; but I shall do it by proxy, friar: your bishop's my friend, and is too honest to let such as you infect a cloister.

GOMEZ
Ay, do, father-in-law, let him be stript of his habit, and disordered.—I would fain see him walk in querpo, like a cased rabbit, without his holy fur upon his back, that the world may once behold the inside of a friar.

Father DOMINICK
Farewell, kind gentlemen; I give you all my blessing before I go.—May your sisters, wives, and daughters, be so naturally lewd, that they may have no occasion for a devil to tempt, or a friar to pimp for them.

[Exeunt, with a **RABBLE** pushing him.

[Enter **TORRISMOND, LEONORA, BERTRAN, RAYMOND, TERESA**, &c.

TORRISMOND
He lives! he lives! my royal father lives!
Let every one partake the general joy.
Some angel with a golden trumpet sound,
King Sancho lives! and let the echoing skies
From pole to pole resound, king Sancho lives!—
Bertran, oh! no more my foe, but brother;
One act like this blots out a thousand crimes.

BERTRAN
Bad men, when 'tis their interest, may do good.
I must confess, I counselled Sancho's murder;
And urged the queen by specious arguments:
But, still suspecting that her love was changed,

I spread abroad the rumour of his death,
To sound the very soul of her designs.
The event, you know, was answering to my fears;
She threw the odium of the fact on me,
And publicly avowed her love to you.

RAYMOND
Heaven guided all, to save the innocent.

BERTRAN
I plead no merit, but a bare forgiveness.

TORRISMOND
Not only that, but favour. Sancho's life,
Whether by virtue or design preserved,
Claims all within my power.

LEONORA
My prayers are heard;
And I have nothing farther to desire,
But Sancho's leave to authorise our marriage.

TORRISMOND
Oh! fear not him! pity and he are one;
So merciful a king did never live;
Loth to revenge, and easy to forgive.
But let the bold conspirator beware,
For heaven makes princes its peculiar care.

[Exeunt.

Footnotes

1. Alluding to the common superstition, that the continuance of the favours of fairies depends upon the receiver's secrecy:—"This is fairy gold, boy, and 'twill prove so: up with it, keep it close; home, home, the nearest way. We are lucky, boy, and, to be so still, requires nothing but secrecy;" Winter's Tale.

2. A red cross, with the words, "Lord have mercy upon us," was placed, during the great plague, upon the houses visited by the disease.

EPILOGUE.

BY A FRIEND OF THE AUTHOR'S.

There's none, I'm sure, who is a friend to love,

But will our Friar's character approve:
The ablest spark among you sometimes needs
Such pious help, for charitable deeds.
Our church, alas! (as Rome objects) does want
These ghostly comforts for the falling saint:
This gains them their whore-converts, and may be
One reason of the growth of popery.
So Mahomet's religion came in fashion,
By the large leave it gave to fornication.
Fear not the guilt, if you can pay for't well;
There is no Dives in the Roman Hell:
Gold opens the strait gate, and lets him in;
But want of money is a mortal sin.
For all besides you may discount to heaven,
And drop a bead to keep the tallies even.
How are men cozened still with shows of good!
The bawd's best mask is the grave friar's hood;
Though vice no more a clergyman displeases,
Than doctors can be thought to hate diseases.
'Tis by your living ill, that they live well,
By your debauches, their fat paunches swell.
'Tis a mock-war between the priest and devil;
When they think fit, they can be very civil.
As some, who did French counsels most advance,
To blind the world, have railed in print at France,
Thus do the clergy at your vices bawl,
That with more ease they may engross them all.
By damning yours, they do their own maintain;
A churchman's godliness is always gain:
Hence to their prince they will superior be;
And civil treason grows church loyalty.
They boast the gift of heaven is in their power;
Well may they give the god, they can devour!
Still to the sick and dead their claims they lay;
For 'tis on carrion that the vermin prey.
Nor have they less dominion on our life,
They trot the husband, and they pace the wife.
Rouse up, you cuckolds of the northern climes,
And learn from Sweden to prevent such crimes.
Unman the Friar, and leave the holy drone
To hum in his forsaken hive alone;
He'll work no honey, when his sting is gone.
Your wives and daughters soon will leave the cells,
When they have lost the sound of Aaron's bells.

John Dryden – A Short Biography

John Dryden was born on August 9th, 1631 in the village rectory of Aldwincle near Thrapston in Northamptonshire, where his maternal grandfather was Rector of All Saints Church.

Dryden was the eldest of fourteen children born to Erasmus Dryden and wife Mary Pickering, paternal grandson of Sir Erasmus Dryden, 1st Baronet (1553–1632) and wife Frances Wilkes, Puritan landowning gentry who supported the Puritan cause and Parliament.

As a boy Dryden lived in the nearby village of Titchmarsh, Northamptonshire where it is probable that he received his first education.

In 1644 he was sent to Westminster School as a King's Scholar where his headmaster was Dr. Richard Busby, a charismatic teacher but severe disciplinarian. Having recently been re-founded by Elizabeth I, Westminster now embraced a very different religious and political spirit encouraging royalism and high Anglicanism but as a humanist public school, it maintained a curriculum which trained pupils in the art of rhetoric and the presentation of arguments for both sides of a given issue. This skill would remain with Dryden and influence his later writing and thinking, as much of it displays these dialectical patterns.

His first published poem, whilst still at Westminster, was an elegy with a strong royalist flavour on the death of his schoolmate Henry, Lord Hastings from smallpox, and alludes to the execution of King Charles I, which took place on January 30th, 1649.

In 1650 Dryden was ready for University and travelled to Trinity College, Cambridge. Dryden's undergraduate years would almost certainly have followed the standard curriculum of classics, rhetoric, and mathematics.

Dryden obtained his BA in 1654, graduating top of the list for Trinity that year.

However family tragedy struck in June of the same year when Dryden's father died, leaving him some land which generated a small income, but not enough to live on.

Returning to London during The Protectorate, Dryden now obtained work with Cromwell's Secretary of State, John Thurloe. This may have been the result of influence exercised on his behalf by his cousin the Lord Chamberlain, Sir Gilbert Pickering.

At Cromwell's funeral on 23 November 1658 Dryden was in the company of the Puritan poets John Milton and Andrew Marvell. The setting was to be a sea change in English history. From Republic to Monarchy and from one set of lauded poets to what would soon become the Age of Dryden.

The start began later that year when Dryden published the first of his great poems, Heroic Stanzas (1658), a eulogy on Cromwell's death which is necessarily cautious and prudent in its emotional display.

With the Restoration of the Monarchy in 1660 Dryden celebrated in verse with Astraea Redux, an authentic royalist panegyric. In this work the interregnum is illustrated as a time of anarchy, and Charles is seen as the restorer of peace and order.

With the king now established Dryden moved quickly to place himself as the leading poet and critic of his day and transferred his allegiances to the new government.

Along with Astraea Redux, Dryden welcomed the new regime with two more panegyrics: To His Sacred Majesty: A Panegyric on his Coronation (1662) and To My Lord Chancellor (1662).

These panegyrics are occasional and written to celebrate events. Thus they are written for the nation rather than the self, but these and others put him in good standing for his eventual appointment as Poet Laureate, where a number of event poems would be required each year and speaking for the Nation and to the Nation would be the first order of duty.

These poems suggest that Dryden was looking to court a possible patron which would have given him an income and time to explore his creative ideas but no, his path instead would be to make a living in writing for publishers, not for the aristocracy, and thus ultimately for the reading public.

In November 1662 Dryden was proposed for membership in the Royal Society, and he was elected an early fellow. However, his inactivity and non payment of dues led to his expulsion in 1666.

On December 1st, 1663 Dryden married the Royalist sister of Sir Robert Howard—Lady Elizabeth Howard (died 1714). The marriage was at St. Swithin's, London, and the consent of the parents is noted on the license, though Lady Elizabeth was then about twenty-five. She was the object of some scandals, well or ill founded; it was said that Dryden had been bullied into the marriage by her brothers. A small estate in Wiltshire was settled upon them by her father. The lady's intellect and temper were apparently not good; her husband was treated as an inferior by those of her social status.

Dryden's works occasionally contain outbursts against the married state but also celebrations of the same. Little else is known of the intimate side of his marriage.

Both Dryden and his wife were warmly attached to their children. They had three sons: Charles (1666–1704), John (1668–1701), and Erasmus Henry (1669–1710). Lady Elizabeth Dryden survived her husband, but went insane soon after his death and died in 1714.

With the re-opening of the theatres after the Puritan ban, Dryden began to also write plays. His first play, The Wild Gallant, appeared in 1663 but was not successful. From 1668 on he was contracted to produce three plays a year for the King's Company, in which he became a shareholder. During the 1660s and '70s, theatrical writing was his main source of income. He led the way in Restoration comedy, his best-known works being Marriage à la Mode (1672), as well as heroic tragedy and regular tragedy, in which his greatest success was All for Love (1678). Dryden was never fully satisfied with his theatrical writings and frequently suggested that his talents were wasted on unworthy audiences.

Certainly therefore fame as a poet looked more rewarding. In 1667, around the same time his dramatic career began, he published Annus Mirabilis, a lengthy historical poem which described the English defeat of the Dutch naval fleet and the Great Fire of London in 1666. It was a modern epic in pentameter quatrains that established him as the pre-eminent poet of his generation, and was crucial in his attaining the posts of Poet Laureate (1668) and then historiographer royal (1670).

When the Great Plague of London closed the theatres in 1665 Dryden retreated to Wiltshire where he wrote Of Dramatick Poesie (1668), arguably the best of his unsystematic prefaces and essays. Dryden constantly defended his own literary practice, and Of Dramatick Poesie, the longest of his critical works, takes the form of a dialogue in which four characters—each based on a prominent contemporary, with Dryden himself as 'Neander'—debate the merits of classical, French and English drama.

He felt strongly about the relation of the poet to tradition and the creative process, and his heroic play Aureng-zebe (1675) has a prologue which denounces the use of rhyme in serious drama. His play All for Love (1678) was written in blank verse, and was to immediately follow Aureng-Zebe.

On December 18th, 1679 he was attacked in Rose Alley near his home in Covent Garden by thugs hired by fellow poet, John Wilmot, 2nd Earl of Rochester, with whom he had a long-standing conflict. Wilmot was constantly in and out of favour with the King and his own poetry was often bawdy, lewd, even obscene and made fun of the King who would often exile him from Court.

Dryden's greatest achievements were in satiric verse: the mock-heroic Mac Flecknoe, a more personal product of his Laureate years, was a lampoon circulated in manuscript and an attack on the playwright Thomas Shadwell. Dryden's main goal in the work is to "satirize Shadwell, ostensibly for his offenses against literature but more immediately we may suppose for his habitual badgering of him on the stage and in print." It is not a belittling form of satire, but rather one which makes his object great in ways which are unexpected, transferring the ridiculous into poetry. This line of satire continued with Absalom and Achitophel (1681) and The Medal (1682). Other major works from this period are the religious poems Religio Laici (1682), written from the position of a member of the Church of England; his 1683 edition of Plutarch's Lives, translated From the Greek by Several Hands in which he introduced the word biography to English readers; and The Hind and the Panther, (1687) which celebrates his conversion to Roman Catholicism.

He wrote Britannia Rediviva celebrating the birth of a son and heir to the Catholic King and Queen on June 10th, 1688. When later in the same year James II was deposed in the Glorious Revolution, Dryden's refusal to take the oaths of allegiance to the new monarchs, William and Mary, which left him out of favour at court and he had to leave his post as Poet Laureate. Thomas Shadwell, his despised rival, succeeded him. Dryden, England's greatest literary figure, was now forced to give up his public offices and live by the proceeds of his pen alone.

Dryden was an excellent translator with his own style which brought the ire of many critics. Many felt he would embellish or expand anything he felt short or curt. Dryden did not feel such expansion was a fault, arguing that as Latin is a naturally concise language it cannot be duly represented by a comparable number of words in the much larger English vocabulary. He continued with his task of translating works by Horace, Juvenal, Ovid, Lucretius, and Theocritus, a task which he found far more satisfying than writing for the stage.

In 1694 he began work on what would be his most ambitious and defining work as translator, The Works of Virgil (1697), which was published by subscription. The publication of the translation of Virgil was a national event and brought Dryden the sum of £1,400.

His final translations appeared in the volume Fables Ancient and Modern (1700), a series of episodes from Homer, Ovid, and Boccaccio, as well as modernised adaptations from Geoffrey Chaucer interspersed with Dryden's own poems. As a translator, he made great literary works in the older languages available to readers of English.

John Dryden died on May 12th, 1700, and was initially buried in St. Anne's cemetery in Soho, before being exhumed and reburied in Westminster Abbey ten days later. He was the subject of poetic eulogies, such as Luctus Brittannici: or the Tears of the British Muses; for the Death of John Dryden, Esq. (London, 1700), and The Nine Muses.

He is seen as dominating the literary life of Restoration England to such a point that the period came to be known in literary circles as the Age of Dryden. Walter Scott called him "Glorious John."

Dryden was the dominant literary figure and influence of his age. He established the heroic couplet as a standard form of English poetry by writing successful satires, religious pieces, fables, epigrams, compliments, prologues, and plays with it; he also introduced the alexandrine and triplet into the form. In his poems, translations, and criticism, he established a poetic diction appropriate to the heroic couplet—Auden referred to him as "the master of the middle style"—that was a model for his contemporaries and for much of the 18th century. The considerable loss felt by the English literary community at his death was evident in the elegies written about him. Dryden's heroic couplet went on to become the dominant poetic form of the 18th century.

What Dryden achieved in his poetry was neither the emotional excitement of the early nineteenth-century romantics nor the intellectual complexities of the metaphysicals. Although he uses formal structures such as heroic couplets, he tried to recreate the natural rhythm of speech, and he knew that different subjects need different kinds of verse. In his preface to Religio Laici he says that "the expressions of a poem designed purely for instruction ought to be plain and natural, yet majestic... The florid, elevated and figurative way is for the passions; for (these) are begotten in the soul by showing the objects out of their true proportion.... A man is to be cheated into passion, but to be reasoned into truth."

Perhaps the following illustrates Dryden and his life—"The way I have taken, is not so streight as Metaphrase, nor so loose as Paraphrase: Some things too I have omitted, and sometimes added of my own. Yet the omissions I hope, are but of Circumstances, and such as wou'd have no grace in English; and the Addition, I also hope, are easily deduc'd from Virgil's Sense. They will seem (at least I have the Vanity to think so), not struck into him, but growing out of him".

John Dryden – A Concise Bibliography

Astraea Redux, 1660
The Wild Gallant (comedy), 1663
The Indian Emperour (tragedy), 1665
Annus Mirabilis (poem), 1667
The Enchanted Island (comedy), 1667, with William D'Avenant from Shakespeare's The Tempest
Secret Love, or The Maiden Queen, 1667
An Essay of Dramatick Poesie, 1668
An Evening's Love (comedy), 1668
Tyrannick Love (tragedy), 1669
The Conquest of Granada, 1670
The Assignation, or Love in a Nunnery, 1672
Marriage à la mode, 1672

Amboyna, or the Cruelties of the Dutch to the English Merchants, 1673
The Mistaken Husband (comedy), 1674
Aureng-zebe, 1675
All for Love, 1678
Oedipus (heroic drama), 1679, an adaptation with Nathaniel Lee of Sophocles' Oedipus
Absalom and Achitophel, 1681
The Spanish Fryar, 1681
Mac Flecknoe, 1682
The Medal, 1682
Religio Laici, 1682
To the Memory of Mr. Oldham, 1684
Threnodia Augustalis, 1685
The Hind and the Panther, 1687
A Song for St. Cecilia's Day, 1687
Britannia Rediviva, 1688, written to mark the birth of a Prince of Wales.
Amphitryon, 1690
Don Sebastian (play), 1690
Creator Spirit, by whose aid, 1690. Translation of Rabanus Maurus' Veni Creator Spiritus
King Arthur, 1691
Cleomenes, 1692
The Art of Satire, 1693
Love Triumphant, 1694
The Works of Virgil, 1697
Alexander's Feast, 1697
Fables, Ancient and Modern, 1700